TERRY FARRELL IN SCOTLAND

TERRY FARRELL

in Scotland

TUCKWELL
PRESS LTD

First published in Great Britain in 2002
by Tuckwell Press Ltd, The Mill House, Phantassie
East Linton EH40 3DG, Scotland

ISBN 1 86232 275 9

British Library Cataloguing-in-Publication Data
A catalogue record for this volume is available on request
from the British Library

Designed and typeset in Quadraat by Dalrymple
Printed and bound in Spain by Book Print SL, Barcelona

Acknowledgements

At Terry Farrell & Partners, the production of this
book was led by Duncan Whatmore, with the essential
assistance of Jane Tobin, and Sir Terry Farrell's
creative overview. The images were selected by
Duncan Whatmore and Jane Tobin, with general text
written by Jane Tobin based on Sir Terry Farrell's
notes, and captions written by Duncan Whatmore.

Special thanks go to Professor Brian Edwards,
Johnny Rodger and Doris Lockhart-Saatchi for their
imaginative and thorough written contributions,
which have been invaluable in providing this book
with critical balance.

The practice also wishes to express its gratitude for
the support of its numerous friends and colleagues in
its second decade in the Edinburgh office. Particular
thanks go to Ian Spence at the City of Edinburgh
Council, Hans Rissmann at EICC, David Crichton at
SEEL and Richard Emerson at Historic Scotland,
for their continual commitment and encouragement.

The patience and diligence of John Tuckwell and
Neville Moir at Tuckwell Press, and Robert Dalrymple
and Nye Hughes at Dalrymple, are gratefully
acknowledged.

Finally, Scotland and the City of Edinburgh –
we thank you for your beauty and inspiration.

Contents

Foreword

Not for a hundred years has a single architect left his mark so indelibly upon the face of Edinburgh. Sir Terry Farrell has been fortunate in the scale of patronage he has received from Scotland's capital city, yet equally Edinburgh has been the recipient of some well conceived, sometimes witty, but always erudite civic interventions. Arguably, Edinburgh is one of Europe's most ordered and picturesque cities. The inheritance of grand squares, handsome streets, public buildings, parks and tenements is without equal. Added to this the topography, landscape and proximity to the sea (or more accurately the Firth of Forth) provides a chemistry rich in picture-postcard imagery and opportunity for the sensitive architect.

Unlike in most other cities, architects and urban designers working in Edinburgh need both a sense of history and occasion. In this arena Farrell is a supremely confident operator: an architect with the necessary sense of theatre and scale and where appropriate lightness of touch, to extract the best out of city sites and developers' briefs.

The projects in this book are of three types – urban masterplans, public buildings, and the adaptation of existing civic structures. Though they span from the urban to the interior scale, the different projects are unified by common concerns. The first and perhaps the defining feature of Farrell's approach is the importance of the public realm. The street and the square, the mall and the promenade of building interiors, celebrate social values. There is a generosity of ambition which acknowledges the importance of the community rather than private interests. Public ambition is expressed in big volumes, in generous proportion, in scale, colour and richness. The practice of Terry Farrell & Partners recognises that complexity is a necessary ingredient for an architecture which has wide appeal. Farrell openly acknowledges Robert Venturi's call to acknowledge the 'importance of the difficult whole' – to create urban projects which play down the dominance of function and celebrate the value of form.

The projects described in detail later also display a recurring interest in geometry. In this they share a fine tradition with earlier architects who have left their mark upon the city of Edinburgh: William Playfair, Gillespie Graham and Robert Adam. These architects like Farrell himself used geometry in plan and section to organise buildings, squares and the landscape itself. The pattern of buildings is not entirely an exterior concern though Farrell is as happy to design the building from the outside in as from the inside out. What he calls positive space is a perennial fascination, or at least the play of positives and negatives acted out in the drama of building volumes and urban space. In this preoccupation one detects a knowledge of urban history which extends beyond the frontiers of Europe to city building in the Middle East and China.

This is not, however, to suggest that Farrell is a classical architect or a revivalist one. He uses the language, construction and methodologies of modernism but joins them to a larger tradition. This takes Farrell back to Edwin Lutyens and John Soane and forward simultaneously to Frank Gehry and Will Alsop. Coloured glass in bold abstract shapes, cantilevered construction and metallic surfaces play a game of contrasts which is knowingly and subtly informed by precedent. In his material compositions Farrell displays a knowledge of contemporary discourse whilst seeking to add to the debate about place and context.

In his recent lectures Terry Farrell has acknowledged his debt to three important architects. The first is Colin Rowe whose analysis of Palladio and later his work with Fred Koetter published in the book *Collage City* has been a recurring influence. *Collage City* brought to public recognition the value of bold geometric urban transplants – pieces of new city which collide and layer themselves into older fabric. Rome gave legitimacy to the kind of urban structuring which recognises old co-ordinates but creates a world of its own – squares, streets and monuments which are modern but play the game of older neighbours. Where the different orders collide, Rowe suggests the geometric consequences add richness and complexity to the whole. In this Farrell has followed not only Rowe's lead but also the precedent of Rome.

The second architect is the Italian Carlo Scarpa whose discreet interventions in historic buildings and landscapes add subtlety and depth. At the Castelvecchio in Verona between 1958 and 1964, Scarpa displayed a sensitivity to ancient walls and space which few modernist architects could match. His approach was craft-based but highly contemporary – contrasting steel, bronze and glass with stone and gnarled timber. The effect was stunning, revealing truth in both worlds – modern and ancient. Farrell too follows the approach though with less fastidiousness and joins it with ideas from Soane to create spaces which, as at the Dean Gallery, have depth and resonance.

The third architect is the contemporary American architect Frank Gehry. Like Farrell himself, Gehry is more concerned with form than function and with the sensuality of building materials rather than their mechanical properties. Gehry has developed an open inclusive architecture which has inspired others and helped elevate architecture back into public consciousness. What Farrell admires is Gehry's urban gestures, particularly his ability to organise external space into a connected sequence of fractured volumes, routes and public monuments.

There are, of course, other influences but Farrell has in his turn been an inspiration to others. It is possible to detect an interest beyond function and beyond narrow definitions of modernity which has been picked up by a younger generation of architects. Theatre, fun, colour and public space are now popular themes in student projects and it is from architects like Farrell, Will Alsop and Zaha Hadid that they take their cues. Architecture is the most public of all the arts, and the manipulation of visual effects joins building design to the fine arts. This is not to suggest that architecture is a form of installation art – its practice, longevity and cost prohibit this. But it does remind us that the roots of architecture lie in art and the academy as much as in science and the laboratory. And Edinburgh is an appropriate city to be reminded of architecture's deep taproot.

Farrell is at the opposite pole to the product design architects who tend in their high tech way to occupy the high ground. His is an open and inclusive approach to urban design which sets buildings and landscape into an ordered whole. To Farrell the masterplan reigns; the role of buildings is to reinforce the containment of space and as a consequence the public interest. In this the orchestration of solid and void relationships is crucial, and often there are positive voids which counterbalance the dominance of corporate interests.

The longevity of streets and squares means that the infrastructure of the city must command more attention. Many of Terry Farrell & Partners' recent projects have been in the area of transport architecture. Here time frames are measured in centuries with impacts occurring across social, economic and cultural realms. In an earlier phase of his professional life Farrell worked under the direction of the transport engineer and planner Sir Colin Buchanan. In his report *Traffic in Towns*, published in 1968, Buchanan argued for a recognition of urban design in dealing with transportation problems. In this Farrell has been an active advocate.

The spaces and voids of the city are where people gather and the drama of life is acted out. Public values require public space and this may conflict with private gain. In his advocacy of masterplan-led regeneration Farrell has, as at Exchange Square in Edinburgh, given prominence to community interests. Here the spaces are positive, the voids deliberately designed for pubic gathering with sun angles, wind, shelter and view carefully considered. It is this choreography of space and volume which marks the Farrell approach. Through urban space the richness and complexity of modern life is acted out for the benefit of all in the city. In setting the ambitions of the private developers into a framework of building volumes, spaces and voids, Farrell has helped protect their investment by ensuring the survival of the social and cultural realm.

DR BRIAN EDWARDS
Professor of Architecture at Edinbugh College of Art, Heriot-Watt University

Edinburgh

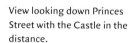

Seen from the vantage point of Edinburgh Castle, central Edinburgh is one of the simplest 'city faces' to understand. Originally a fortified settlement built on a rocky outcrop and surrounded by low-lying land, over time it has come to comprise four elements: the Old Town, spreading from the Castle down the Royal Mile to the Palace of Holyrood; the Nor' (or North) Loch – or gardens in a valley, as they are now – with the railway lines that run through it; the linear New Town; and the Firth of Forth, visible in the distance.

The constricted nature of the Old Town meant that opportunity for expansion was limited – so, from the late eighteenth century, the Neoclassical New Town was built on flat land almost half a mile from the Old Town, linked by striking elevated bridges spanning the Loch, which was then drained and landscaped. At the fringe of the New Town runs the irregular Water of Leith, which winds through a gorge before reaching the Forth. Each element – the Old Town, the Loch (or gardens), the New Town and the Firth of Forth –

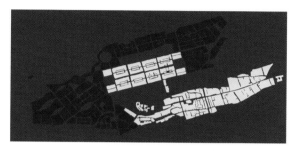

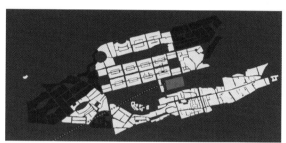

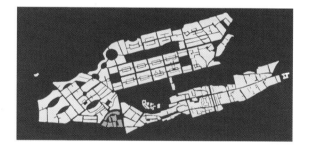

The stages of Edinburgh's development: Old Town, New Town, arrival of the railway and, most recently, TFP's International Conference Centre and Financial District masterplan on Lothian Road, linking Old and New Towns.

View looking down Princes Street with the Castle in the distance.

runs east–west in a four-layered sequence. It is a
sublime composition, making Edinburgh truly one
of the great cities of the world.

Edinburgh's ordered core belies a disordered
perimeter. The city centre embraces a philosophi-
cal Enlightenment vision of the urban ideal, whose
wealth was dependent on its hidden opposite: the
vast, chaotic, dynamic and fragmented industrial
suburbs that are etched far into the landscape, and
that eventually reach out towards Edinburgh's age-
old rival, Glasgow.

The city's diversity is reflected in Terry Farrell &
Partners' Edinburgh projects, where the picturesque setting of the Dean Gallery, adjacent to the
Water of Leith, is seen to evoke a very distinct
architectural response from the urban location of
the Conference Centre and Sheraton Spa.

▲
Aerial view showing the
Castle looking towards the
gridded New Town.

The Exchange Financial
District Masterplan

The Exchange Financial District Masterplan

◄

The Caledonian Railway Station with associated goods yard and track infrastructure formed a key junction between the Old and New Towns. The barrier imposed by the track into the station from the west would become sustained by the construction of the West Approach Road on the same route. The shaded area shows the area of the TFP's masterplan.

The 4.2-hectare site, located in west-central Edinburgh on former railway lands that included the Caledonian railway station, offered the potential for a significant inner-city development.

Edinburgh has an inspired tradition of careful and skilful town planning that has resulted in a harmonious juxtaposition of organic medieval street patterns and ordered Georgian planning. However, this harmony had been marred by the building of the Caledonian railway station in 1870 at a point where the Old Town meets the New, and which acted as a significant barrier between the New Town and the triangle of land between Lothian Road and Morrison Street.

TFP's masterplan heals this divide by re-establishing links across the former railway land to the New Town, at the same time restoring an appropriate urban grain and density for the area. The new quarter is designed to extend the city of Edinburgh to the west: TFP's masterplan opens up land that, for the most part, has been inaccessible to the public for a century.

The Exchange Financial District masterplan was the first major British commission undertaken by TFP outside London. Won in competition in 1989, the commission drew on Terry Farrell's enthusiasm for 'gentle architecture', a theme evident in his earliest work. In 1984, Farrell wrote in a practice monograph: "'Gentle architecture' implies that which is accessible to a wide range of people; is non-alienating in contextual handling and external expression of internal use and entrance ways; is unassertive and familiar in colour, form, imagery and formality of arrangement, sane and humane in terms of non-extreme theoretical or technological interpretations; and is above all an anxiety-free

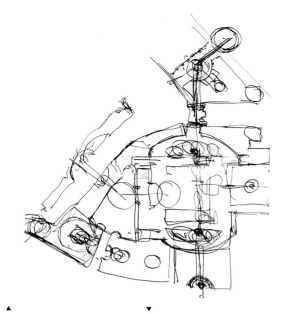

▲

A pair of new public squares was conceived as the armature for organising the buildings and patterns of movement around them. The provision of servicing infrastructure at basement level allows cyclists and pedestrians unchallenged access to the upper spaces.

▼

A continuity with the tradition of linked organised formal spaces in the New Town and West End is established over the West Approach Road – previously the route taken by the railway into the Caledonian Station. The road has been realigned to follow the subterranean Waverley track route, allowing two constraints to the development above to be unified and thence diminished.

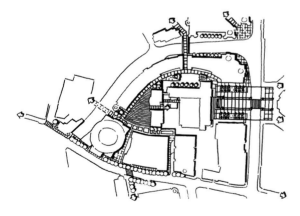

►

Edinburgh, as particularly with many Northern British cities, expresses its urban and topographical character through silhouette. An exploration of the Exchange's impact on this distinct layered skyline was an essential early study in gauging the masterplan's contribution to the perception of the city.

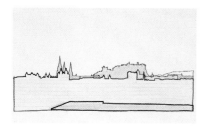

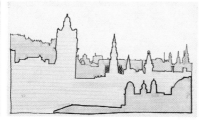

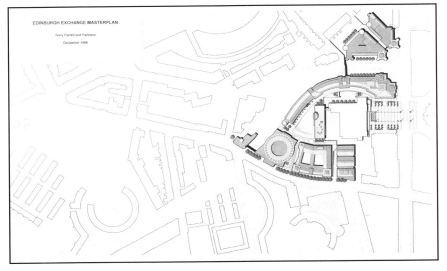

EDINBURGH EXCHANGE MASTERPLAN

Terry Farrell and Partners

December 1999

routes and car-parking facilities.

The distinctive drum-like form of the Edinburgh International Conference Centre, completed in 1995, landmarks the site and forms a setpiece within the urban mass. Reflecting the differing needs of those who work, visit and stay on the site, the TFP scheme accommodates a mixture of uses, including office and conference facilities, retail space, leisure facilities and car parking, as well as carefully integrating the existing Sheraton Hotel.

Drawing on the city's vernacular tradition of terraces and crescents enclosing urban spaces and gardens, the building blocks are set up in a gently sweeping curve that defines the site envelope. At the heart of the project is the triangular Conference Square, which forms the main public space for the Conference Centre. Nearby is a diversity of public spaces and walkways that resemble public rooms and corridors within a building. Rather than providing an impersonal expanse with buildings around the edge, TFP's masterplan incorporates elements of contrast and surprise. For example, the angular Sheraton Spa, squeezed into an uncompromisingly small plot of land, provides a startling visual juxtaposition with the circular Conference Centre. Likewise, the intimate footpath that comprises the crescent opens up into the grand space of Conference Square.

Creating a tangible public domain for pedestrians is central to the masterplan – its success

▲

As the masterplan became implemented it continued to evolve, with subtle adjustments to the buildings' footprints and location of specific uses informing the character of the linking spaces. Each new development was able to be influenced by and add to the cumulative whole.

architecture which doesn't feed off any crisis cultivation'.

Drawing on lessons learned from masterplans for other London developments such as King's Cross railway lands, Tobacco Dock and Charing Cross, and the masterplan for Comyn Ching Triangle, Covent Garden, the scheme reflects Edinburgh's great tradition of city planning.

The masterplan provides plots for seven office developments and a leisure pavilion arranged around three public spaces – Conference Square, Festival Square and the Morrison Street entrance to the Conference Centre – incorporating pedestrian

▶

The distinctive pattern of axial streets and crescents in the West End is extrapolated and reinterpreted as a template for the Exchange, providing a permeable, accessible public realm. The squares, crescents and circuses of the New Town supply the precedent for the visual impact of spaces set within an urban grid, but these have not usually been freely accessible.

▲

Building forms within and around the Exchange announce their civic status and add to the texture of the city, often complementing other established uses. New synergies between previously unconnected uses are emerging.

Approaching completion, the Exchange has generated a cascade of fringe developments and has become firmly rooted into its context. Its boundary is becoming increasingly difficult to recognise: the Exchange is now an integrated part of the city rather than a distinct district.

depends on good ground-level connection. Urban development that strives to accommodate motorised traffic, together with the fracture between past and present, has made Edinburgh a less enjoyable place for pedestrians. The quality of the pedestrian domain relies on the design and form of individual buildings.

Within the Exchange, extensive pedestrian and cycle routes form connections with existing streets beyond the site. Conference Square and Festival Square are linked by the crescent, and in this way the Conference Centre is directly linked to the Sheraton Hotel and Usher Hall, as well as to the West End and the New Town via a new pedestrian bridge and Rutland Square. Internal spaces and the areas around buildings are regarded as equally important.

The driving forces behind the Edinburgh masterplan are historical continuity, the integration of old and new, pedestrian access, and the quest for richness and diversity. Terry Farrell and Partners' singular concept of urban design allows an incremental approach that encourages the area to take shape in its own way. Confronting the reality of the urban situation – rather than prescribing utopian visions – is an integral part of TFP's outlook.

Exchange Financial District:
Festival Square

◄

The relocation of the West Approach Road further to the north permitted the third edge of Festival Square to be developed. This frames the Usher Hall as an axial setpiece and provides the opportunity for linked activities within the new space created across Lothian Road.

▼ ►

Natural materials, including large Caithness stone flags and granite slabs and cubes, signature lighting, pleached lime trees and low hedging, provide visual and spatial continuity with other elements of the masterplan.

▲

A judicious mix of building
types and uses around the
perimeter of Festival Square
ensures a range of activity –
from pedestrians and cyclists
moving into the other
connected spaces of the
Exchange, to activity associated with the bars and
restaurants at the north and
west edges.

▲

Lighting, water and trees help to structure an accessible public space, poised to become a new platform for activities during and beyond the Festival. An exhaustive selection process led to the commissioning of a work of art that uses water and sculptural forms to provide a focus to the square.

Exchange Financial District:
The Edinburgh International Conference Centre

APPRAISAL BY DR BRIAN EDWARDS

(courtesy of the *Architects' Journal*)

Farrell's buildings are generally a powerful statement and the Edinburgh International Conference Centre is no exception, for he has an uncanny knack of exploiting civic procession, vista and urban scale. In many ways, a large conference centre is the perfect vehicle to relay Farrell's thesis of the interconnectedness of public and private space, and interior and exterior volumes. In theory, Edinburgh is the ideal canvas for his architecture with the city's clarity of structure and ordered relationship of monument and terrace matching Farrell's own urban design thesis.

Edinburgh has few pockets of inner-city dereliction, and it is on one of them that Farrell's conference centre has become the focal point of a plan of offices, hotels and shops which follow the morphology of Edinburgh by adopting terraces, crescents and squares as the structuring device.

Anchored at one end, and providing the punctuation to existing streets, the conference centre effectively handles the transition between newly grafted urban tissue and older, mainly Georgian, streets. Between an earlier 1989 masterplan and the implemented scheme, Farrell was given the opportunity to move the conference centre from its position on Lothian Road to Morrison Street; a wise move which allows a smooth progression, physically

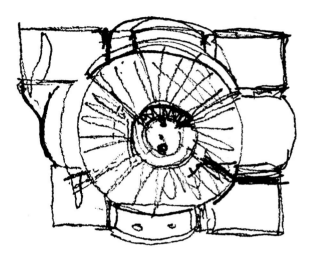

▲
Design development sketch by Terry Farrell indicating the early aspiration for a radial organisation of the building's form. This wheel and hub arrangement benefited circulation, as well as the structural rationale for spanning large spaces.

▼
Design development sketches. The forms of the building – particularly the massive drum and street-scale pavilions – are emerging, as are the principle of a circular ordering motif and a glazed entrance. Further studies would develop cladding systems, expressing themes being explored in the interaction of interior volumes.

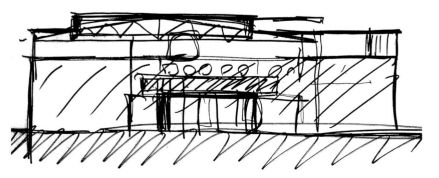

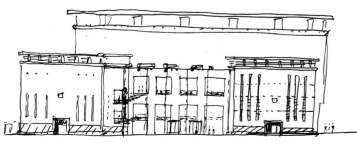

An early Terry Farrell sketch demonstrates the contrast between the civic scale of the drum and the tenemental scale of the corner pavilions

and entrance. The latter re-establish the dialogue with Morrison Street in both height and alignment with existing buildings opposite.

The dramatic juxtaposition of plane and curve allows the building's presence to remain legible from a variety of angles and distances. Even a glimpse of a small segment of the roof allows the Conference Centre's full span to be extrapolated and perceived.

and socially, from old to new. It also allowed the conference centre to become a major landmark along the important Western Approach Road.

Farrell is primarily an urban architect, and the landscape of ideas he manipulates is not about buildings but cities. His buildings are generally grandly conceived and boldly executed parcels of urban surgery. Like Nash, whom he admires, Farrell approaches the architectural problem from the point of view of space in and around buildings. It is essentially space which orders his urban plans and helps establish the relationship between volumes outside and within buildings, and which is

the material he uses to join new and old city fabric. Space too is the main medium of expression with solid, not transparent, walls as the defining element. Unlike Koolhaas and Alsop, who also exploit bigness, Farrell avoids abrupt clashes of scale or architectural culture. His buildings though large mediate between often disconnected urban landscapes.

The conference centre follows most of Farrell's central tenets, yet it marks a slight departure, particularly from his London projects. Vauxhall Cross and Alban Gate are buildings gesturing to the city while serving mainly corporate, private ideals. In Edinburgh, a new landmark is justified by the public nature of the building. In this he is following a fine lineage in the city.

As external spectacle, Farrell leaves little doubt that this is a civic structure. The architectural language of the solid masonry wall, the lofty and inviting entrance way, the rotunda rising forcefully and elegantly above the slated rooftops, and the great oversailing cornice, all testify to a new public monument.

▲ ▼
The relationships between the massive drum, corner pavilions, glazed entrance area and canopy were explored in model form, as was the dialogue between the edges of the pavilions and the adjacent street lines. A rigorous geometric system ordering the drum and giving rise to the calibrated lens, signifying rotation, allowed the pavilions to lock on at cardinal points.

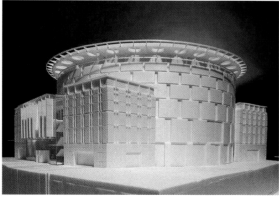

The Conference Centre's main auditorium can be subdivided from a 1200-seat space to two 300-seat spaces and one 600-seat space, or one 900- and one 300-seat space. The moving walls of the small auditoria echo the exterior architecture of the outside drum of the Conference Centre.

Entrance level plan. Rotary circulation is encouraged (as on all levels above ground) around the perimeter of the drum, returning to the glazed entrance canopy for vertical movement via lift, stairs and escalator. Access into the building can be achieved from north, south and east, to suit the requirements of the building's internal programme.

Auditorium-level plan, showing one smaller revolving auditorium engaged with the principal space, the other rotated round to address its own stage. Circulation and access are designed to service both arrangements. Entry to the main auditorium from the foyer takes place through the structural hub of the building.

There are hints too that building technology should not be hidden but expressed. Construction, particularly of the entrance portico, carries the candour and daring associated with more avant-garde design. The effect is to introduce complexity and surprise, particularly at street level, with steel, fabric canopies and etched glass layered against the stone walls with some delicacy. The steel cornice does much the same thing for the rotunda, adding a ring of coloured light at night.

To drive along the Western Approach Road and see the changing geometry of stone rotunda and circular perforated cornice is to be reminded of Farrell's perennial interest in skyline. The play of inter-locking circles and repeating, rhyming elements links, conceptually at least, the inside of the building – with its plans of big and small circles – to the outside.

Inevitably, for an architect who thrives on grand urban gestures, the conference centre has a circular auditorium. The circle inside immediately justifies the rotunda shape which climbs above Edinburgh's rooftops. Rather like the Royal Festival Hall, the basic shape of the auditorium rises through the lower floors to break out in celebratory fashion at roof level. Like the Usher Hall nearby on Lothian Road, the Edinburgh Conference Centre uses the volume of the auditorium to signal not just the primary use but to organise the various entrances around its edge.

Farrell's design skilfully maintains the line of streets at ground level by creating four pavilions at each corner. These rise to about the level of adjoining tenements and follow the curving lines of older

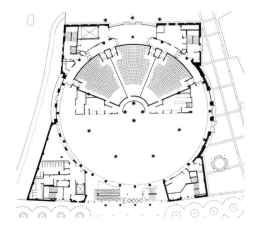

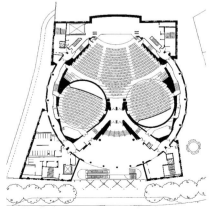

The drum and its oversailing cantilevered roof edge provide many metaphors for movement and rotation, signalling the internal volumes and their moveable configuration. These shapes are anchored by the static rectilinear stone pavilions, allowing the drum to become embedded in its urban matrix.

Cross section with Conference Square on the right and Morrison Street on the left. The three principal layers within the drum (auditorium, ground floor, exhibition hall) are augmented by more cellular service spaces (access corridors, toilets, committee rooms, projection and simultaneous interpretation booths, technical and plant rooms) grouped around the perimeter of the drum and in the pavilions.

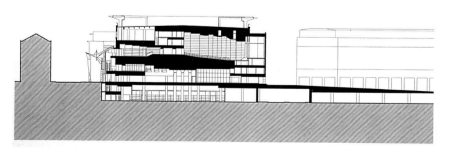

streets. They have the effect of cementing the building into its immediate context while allowing the more fragmentary views of the rotunda to perform city-wide identification. Subtly too, the design of the pavilions with their lofty floor heights and horizontally banded slots of windows refer to the Georgian traditions nearby.

Farrell is a designer who enjoys scale. Embankment Place, which sits above Charing Cross Station and is arguably his best London project, is a building whose presence derives from the considered relationship between the architectural elements and the Thames. He tends to move upwards in scale when opportunities present themselves, recognising that scale is not just a question of size.

This is evident at the conference centre in the layering of the drum, which gives the rotunda a visual force lacking in the pavilions. Distorted storey-height bands of stone with windows which reduce in height give the impression of a larger building. The classical language, particularly in the hands of Ledoux or 'Greek' Thomson, provide possible precedents.

There is a hint of Ledoux in the basic geometry of the building. His Barriere de la Villette in Paris employs a similar composition of central rotunda, with corner pavilions and a boldly expressed entrance portico. Interestingly, Ledoux's building is as much civic ornament as an expression of interior function. From Thomson too one can see the play of horizontal and vertical articulation which though classical in inspiration, is still decidedly tectonic.

The progression from street to auditorium seat is a smooth play of changing, mainly circular, volumes. The clarity of plan is not overly compromised by safety and security considerations. Escalators and staircases taken along the Morrison Street frontage allow both interior and exterior views to be enjoyed simultaneously. A large reception hall of ample height and rather Art Deco detailing provides a place to gather before attending a conference. It has the sense of occasion needed to ensure that on television it will provide an appropriate backcloth for a political convention.

Compared to other conference centres this is a building with scale and gravitas. Unlike the

Stone for the corner pavilions was selected to match, in colour, texture and consistency, the buff Craigleith stone quarried locally to construct Edinburgh's New Town. Curved panels of precast concrete are of a suitable scale to express the drum's presence as a civic object.

The distinctive roof and the drum cladding follow a rigorous ordering geometry which determines many of the building's elements, from the location of structure, windows, corner pavilions, internal spaces, down to the arrangement of doors, partitions and even light fittings.

conference centres in Harrogate and Birmingham, with their rather glitzy imagery and mainly transparent exteriors, this building is more solemn though at times slightly exotic.

The nearest parallel in terms of architectural ambition is the Queen Elizabeth Conference Centre in London by Powell and Moya. This too is a building that has to address urban as well as architectural aspirations, though the need in London was rather more for a dignified facade to overlook the end of Parliament Square than a re-profiling of the capital's skyline.

Like all the practice's more important buildings, the Conference Centre exploits the tension between architecture, landscape and urban design. There is the sense that the grand gesture and the ad hoc are joint conspirators in the creation of some of Britain's most publicly popular buildings of the past decade. The combining of heavy and light construction, and of colour and whiteness creates a building which cannot easily be overlooked.

Farrell is not a simple architect. To paraphrase Venturi, he adopts a responsibility towards the difficult whole. He seems to be an architect who has much the same relationship to building as opera does to music. To judge the Edinburgh Conference Centre as a building alone is to miss the point of the other compositional factors which contribute so much to the experience.

One of these factors is undoubtedly humour, for who but Farrell would have the nerve to place a great Roman Coliseum in the Athens of the North? Who would have the courage to design a rotunda within the rectilinear grid of central Edinburgh and then to celebrate with a blue halo?

Exchange Financial District: Sheraton Grand Hotel Spa

◄

The design concept for the building's envelope is a balance of transparency, translucency and opacity that creates layers and depth within the facades, simultaneously screening and revealing the interiors.

▼

Early concept computer rendering. The 'fish tail' is still in embryonic form and occupies most of the length of the façade, and is yet to dramatically emerge proud of the cladding, expressing the hydropool within.

Terry Farrell & Partners developed the external expression for the Sheraton Spa, responding to the Syntax Group's concepts of internal spatial and volumetric design. A coordinated and integrated approach to colour and materials led to the UK's first stand-alone urban health spa – a unique centrepiece that completes the TFP-designed Exchange masterplan.

The completion of the Spa allows TFP's masterplan for the new Exchange district to be experienced as a legible piece of the city for the first time. Centred on two significant new urban spaces, the Exchange masterplan links the Old to the New Town with a dense flow of new pedestrian and cycle paths that conceal a labyrinth of existing infrastructure and vehicle routes. Drawing freely from the planning traditions of the New Town, where terrace and crescent enclose urban space, the masterplan establishes a gently sweeping curve of buildings that define the edge of the development while providing enclosure for the new public spaces within.

Through the Exchange masterplan, won in competition in 1989, TFP have realised a significant piece of urban design. Landmarked by the Inter-

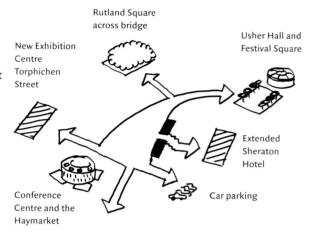

Rutland Square across bridge

New Exhibition Centre Torphichen Street

Usher Hall and Festival Square

Extended Sheraton Hotel

Conference Centre and the Haymarket

Car parking

▲

Drawing showing location of the Spa building within Conference Square and its permeability to local amenities.

▼

Concept sketch by Terry Farrell, exploring the palette of materials and their relationship with the building's internal functions.

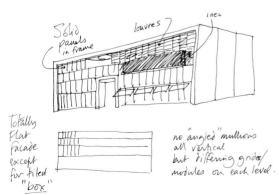

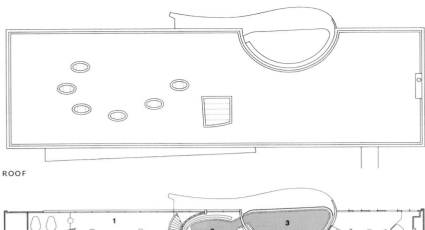

ROOF

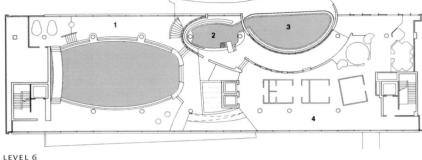

LEVEL 6

LEVEL 4

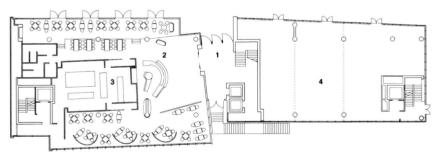

LEVEL 3

LEVEL 3 PLAN KEY	LEVEL 4 PLAN KEY	LEVEL 6 PLAN KEY
1 Entrance Foyer	1 Aerobics	1 Pool Hall
2 Restaurant	2 Gym	2 Internal Spa Pool
3 Kitchen	3 Therapy Suites	3 External Spa Pool
4 Retail		4 Thermal Suite

national Conference Centre (completed by TFP in 1995) and striking new Spa building, the masterplan provides plots for seven large office developments arranged around three distinctive public spaces and thoroughfares. Built on a large tract of disused railway land, the Exchange heals a rift that once isolated large parts of the inner city from the West End. A cascade of regeneration and development activity to the south and west is a tangible sign of the success of the masterplan in removing the barriers that for so long divided this part of the city.

Right from the start, the site for the Sheraton Spa was conceived to be the visual and pivotal heart of the masterplan – in Terry Farrell's words, it is the 'final piece of the jigsaw'. Juxtaposed with the circular Conference Centre and the curving lines of the site envelope, the Spa stands out as a startlingly linear concrete and glass pavilion. Enclosed on four sides by heavy-looking stone-clad buildings, it fits into the restricted site with lightness and precision. Linking the Conference Centre and Spa is the triangular-shaped Conference Square, a new pedestrianised space that fronts the Spa's west (entrance) elevation and sits neatly on top of a two-storey car park.

As masterplanners, TFP conceived the core of this pivotal site to be a mixed-use, inherently urban building. The round-the-clock nature of the Spa, with its intensity of use and variety of programme, perfectly fitted this requirement. Its restaurant/bar, cafe, retail and spa elements offer a multiple-occupancy building with a range of different but complementary environments based around health and leisure. Working in collaboration with interior architects Syntax, the building is designed to encourage liveliness and activity, with each use planned as a discreet individual entity within the overall whole.

The four-storey building sets the boundary of Conference Square and brings activity to this new public space. Sitting on top of two levels of car parking, the Spa establishes a new ground level that feeds into and completes the Exchange by complementing the organisational layout of the Conference Centre and surrounding crescent buildings.

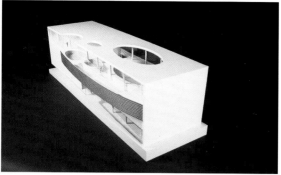

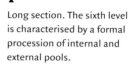

Long section. The sixth level is characterised by a formal procession of internal and external pools.

The 4,900-square-metre building houses internal and external pools, hydrotherapy and beauty suites, a gymnasium, exercise studios, restaurant, bar and associated retail space. A defining element in the planning of the Spa is the internal street, which maximises the intensity of uses. This runs horizontally through the centre of the building, connecting the east and west elevations, and vertically from the basement car park to the four storeys above. Either side of the street, the floor plan is segmented into two halves. Emphasising this, and creating further diversity, subdivision

Study models of the Sheraton Spa. More vigorous modelling of the rectilinear form's contrasting organic shapes is evident, as is an exploration of the penetration of natural light into the building, particularly through the roof and glazed areas.

◄

Cross section highlighting the bridge link to the Sheraton Hotel.

KEY

1 Thermal Suite	5 Retail
2 External Spa Pool	6 Car Park
3 Changing	7 Conference Square
4 Therapy Suites	8 Service Road

◄

Long section showing the car park located in an undercroft below the Spa building. The building's floor plates rise independently of the north-south orientation.

KEY

1 Thermal Suite	7 Retail
2 Pool Hall	8 Restaurant
3 Changing	9 Car Park
4 Club Lounge	10 Plant
5 Aerobics	11 Entrance Foyer
6 Therapy Suites	12 Service Road

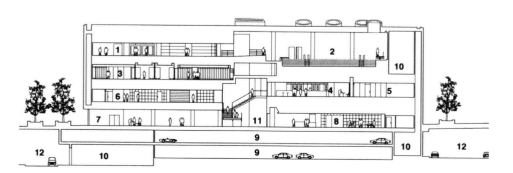

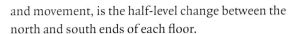

▶
Exploded axonometric
describing the vertical flow of
space from the car park, up
through the public level at
Conference Square and into
the Spa itself.

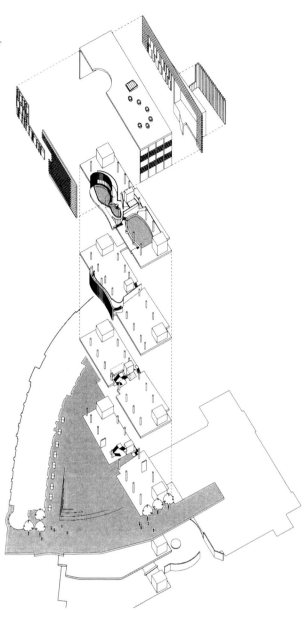

and movement, is the half-level change between the north and south ends of each floor.

At ground level, the retail outlet is positioned at the north-west entrance to Conference Square from the walkway, while the restaurant sits at the building's south-west end, connecting with the Square. Both spaces function as individual volumes within the whole. Levels one and two contain car parking; level three – the entrance level – also houses retail and the restaurant; level four contains the aerobics area, the gym and therapy suites; level five is the changing area and contains the bridge link to the Sheraton Hotel; and level six houses the pools and thermal suite. The result is maximum connectivity and efficiency of circulation.

The architecture of the Spa is designed to capitalise on its compact setting, and its jubilant palette of colour and materials can be glimpsed from various points around the masterplan, enticing the visitor through the perimeter buildings and into the core of the site. The sense of light, space and weightlessness of the elevations contrasts dramatically with the surrounding stone façades and provides a clear indication of the building's role as a place for leisure, relaxation and the promotion of good health.

The Spa is designed as a series of opposites engaged in a constant state of play: horizontal and vertical; solid and void; angular and curved; translucency and transparency; movement and stasis; weightlessness and rootedness. A key expression of this play of opposites is the three-dimensional representation of internal elements on the exterior façades – such as the restaurant and the exuberant 'fish tail'. This swoosh of pearlescent aluminium houses an external hydrotherapy pool and cuts in and out of the spa's rectangular volume. Its interior face is scooped out of the glazing, like a ribbon turned back on itself, and is clad in soft-coloured

▼
West (front) and east (back)
elevations.

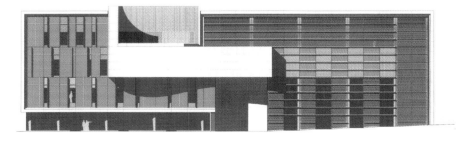

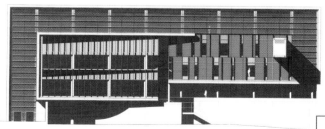

Iroko boarding. The timber soffit becomes a canopy for the double-height entrance below as it sweeps into the internal street – a cleft in the building's centre. Cutting a cave-like fissure through the rectangular volume, the entrance offsets the bright openness of the carved-out hydrotherapy pool and provides a counterpoint to the fish tail above.

The overall rectangular form, the blue/green vitrified-ceramic fritted glass and the off-white concrete framing motif link what would otherwise be two quite different façades. Able to articulate both translucency and transparency, the fritted glass gives users appropriate levels of openness and privacy. Light and shade are moderated through subtle variations in the fritting on both east and west elevations. This distinguishes between private or secluded spaces and public areas. The transparency causes the elevations to change colour dramatically as light moves about the building, which in turn creates a dynamic influence on its surrounds. During Edinburgh's

dark winter days, the building is transformed into a glowing lantern, infusing warmth into the new district.

The unifying off-white concrete frame, encapsulating the principal edges of the two elevations, is interlocked by a smaller sub-frame on the east elevation, which contains the glazed face of the bar area. Delineating the points of weightlessness and rootedness, the concrete frame emphasises the monolithic plinth on which the building rests. The plinth plays a key role in articulating ideas of weightlessness, stability and balance, as well as the change of plane on the east elevation, where the gymnasium and bar area seemingly expand to form a wedge of space that pushes out of the glazing.

The Spa is an example of architecture integrated into its urban setting. It is a building that seeks to exploit the minimum of form, materials and colour to maximum potential. The aim of the architecture is to bring richness and diversity into a new part of the city by becoming a colourful focal point and place-maker in its own right.

▲

The thin skin of precast concrete forms the end elevation and drops to touch the ground at this edge of the building.

SHERATON GRAND HOTEL SPA
APPRAISAL BY JOHNNY RODGER

Sited behind the Sheraton Hotel and forming the eastern edge of Conference Square, this building is constructed over the two storeys of car parking under the Square. Accommodation includes two rooftop swimming pools, hydrotherapy and beauty suites, gymnasia and exercise rooms, bars, restaurants and retail space. TFP completed the shell of the building by 2000, and the interior fit-out by Syntax was completed in summer 2001.

A concrete-and-glass walled box, it comes as a relief from the heaviness of all the surrounding neo-classical facades and enlivens Conference Square in a way that is entirely unexpected. It charges into a tight and very uncompromising site, its northern concrete and louvred wall coming within 12 metres of the Clydesdale Plaza facade to form the apex of the roughly triangular public space.

The proximity of stone facades would be unwelcoming, not to say threatening, to pedestrians approaching that opening to the Square were it not for the clever way the off-rectilinear geometry of the building has been handled. The ground floor is completely glass-walled, with accommodation for shops and bars and the concrete box overhangs this so that pedestrians have visual access through the building to the irregularly shaped and sloped Conference Square opening out in front of them.

▼
The bridge link enables guests of the Sheraton Hotel to move internally between the two buildings.

▼
The pool hall is bathed in horizontal blades of light, filtered through the blue ceramic fritted glass panels which provide the building with its distinctive translucent skin.

▲
Foaming water, warm and slightly saline, spouts from rooftop jets along the edge of the external hydropool, ensuring the comfort of bathers enjoying the city's panorama.

▼◄
The upper levels of the building are illuminated through the glazed walls and elliptical rooflights piercing the otherwise solid ceiling, giving a lazy curve for backstroking swimmers to follow. Privacy and calm are not compromised even by a glimpse of the bustling Exchange Financial District outside.

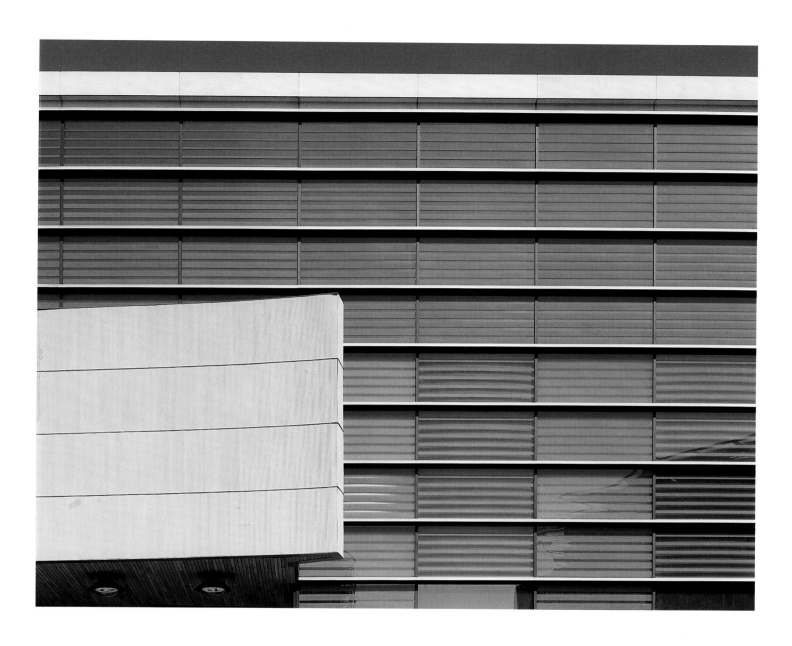

▲

The west elevation showing the fritted glass detail, creating an architecture of glass, colour and light.

A part of the main Sheraton Hotel complex which lies to its east, the building communicates via a glass bridge on the top floor and steps from the Spa entrance hall down to the Hotel's main road entrance. The Health Club does, however, maintain its own identity, and the form and palette of materials combine to give it a light, transparent, aquatic style. Both east and west facades are completely glazed with blue and green ceramic fritting providing shade, colour and play of light. The fish-shaped curve of the feature containing the outdoor pool cantilevers out from the upper storey clad in a microrib of mica flip finish which looks brown/grey in shade but has a scaly blue green aquatic shimmer in the sun.

This building can be placed as part of Farrell's modernist experimentation which took in such other glass-walled projects as his retail and clinic buildings for Korea. Yet there's more to it than that. Once inside we find that the heavy concrete pillars and the stepped section of the floors not only contribute to the effect of the play of light, but clearly are involved in some special promenade. We go round concrete pillars, up ramps and steps, across gymnasia, passing sequestered therapy rooms, through the cat flap to the outdoor heated

▲

The curved wall of the rooftop outdoor pool.

pool. We find ourselves in some neo-Roman baths here with all the classical order of their promenade: frigidarium, tepidarium, caldarium, palestrae, etc. The similarity in plan between the Baths of Caracalla in Rome, with their caldarium rotunda protruding on the long side and opening up the centrally planned rectangle, and this Health Club with its hot outdoor pool cantilevered out from the top floor, is striking.

But perhaps we ought not to be surprised to find this thoroughly researched basis to one of Farrell's ostensibly stylised buildings. As Duncan Whatmore (in charge of Farrell's Edinburgh office) says of the evolution of their architecture: 'we think of it as different analytical processes rather than different styles'. That seems a mature approach, but as masterplanners is it too much to ask of other design architects?

The Dean Gallery and Masterplan

The Dean Gallery and Masterplan

◄ A new gravel forecourt provides the Dean Gallery with a 'country house' setting in keeping with its grand façade.

► Aerial view. The Dean is characterised by its two Baroque-style chimney towers.

Before embarking on the redesign of the nineteenth-century Dean Orphanage, Terry Farrell & Partners were required to reshape the landscape into an appropriate setting for an art gallery. The idea behind the landscape design was to draw upon and emphasise the contrast between the rational grid layout of Edinburgh's Old Town and the picturesque system that defined the New Town.

The aim was to create an area of rambling parkland with pedestrian links between the Dean Gallery and the National Gallery of Modern Art. The site plan also encompassed the Dean Cemetery, a necropolis in Victorian style containing Edinburgh's richest collection of memorials, including three by William Playfair (one was for himself).

► View of the area's 'pauper palaces' from 1859. In the centre is Hamilton's Dean; to its left is John Watson's Institution, now the Scottish National Gallery of Modern Art and to the right is Daniel Stewart's Hospital. The fourth 'pauper palace', Donaldson's Orphan School, designed by William Playfair, is not shown.

Serpentine paths connect the garden spaces with the adjacent Water of Leith walkway – a beautiful route following the wooded banks of the ravine where the river passes through the New Town – and other routes leading to other parts of the city. A further attraction is a landform designed in conjunction with Charles Jencks and based on one that he and the late Maggie Keswick had in their garden in Portrack, Dumfriesshire. This layout aims to provide the visitor with a synthesis of art and nature, as was the Picturesque way.

In order to obtain the tranquillity characteristic of a Picturesque garden, all car parking has been sited north of the Dean Gallery's back elevation, leaving an area of undisturbed parkland to the south. This also applies to the National Gallery of Modern Art: previously, vehicles crossed in front of the Gallery, obscuring the view of the main elevation. An allotment garden – formerly the Orphanage kitchen garden – has been reinstated.

Extracting a rich and layered cultural and historical narrative from the existing Grade A listed building constructed by Thomas Hamilton in 1831–33, TFP aimed to stimulate the senses by a clever interplay between juxtaposition, games playing and historical context.

The Dean's future as an arts building was assured in 1995, when the National Galleries of Scotland (NGS) decided to relocate their extensive works of art stored at The Mound. Then, Leith-born

▼ Concept sketch by Terry Farrell.

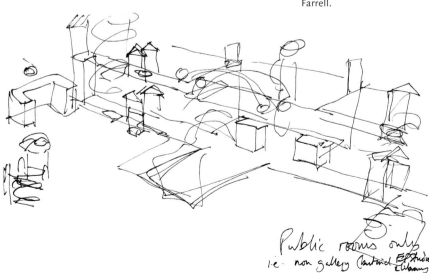

▶

Analysis drawings of the three primary components comprising Thomas Hamilton's historic Dean building.

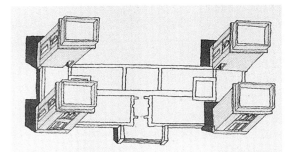

FOUR CORNER PAVILIONS

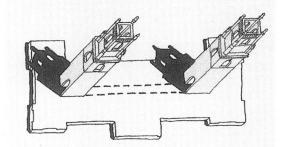

TWIN TOWERS ORDER BUILDING

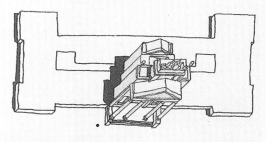

CENTRAL 'TEMPLE' ON AXIS

▶

Concept sketches by Terry Farrell exploring ways to restore the building to its original grandeur.

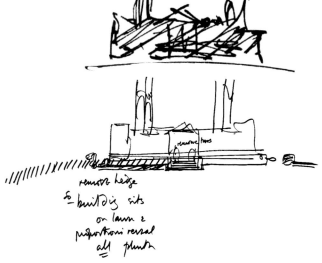

sculptor Eduardo Paolozzi bequeathed his collection to the NGS, alongside gifts by the Dada and Surrealist collectors Roland Penrose and Gabrielle Keiller. At the same time, the NGS were searching for a new headquarters, and it was thought that the converted Dean would provide an ideal home. However, even if it had been used to accommodate the NGS stores, the bequests and the administration centre, the Dean would still not have been used to maximum capacity, so the idea arose of including in the design galleries for temporary exhibitions.

In addition to Thomas Hamilton's existing building and a multifaceted client brief, TFP were handed a patchwork of legacies. The practice sought to weave a three-dimensional tapestry incorporating Hamilton, Paolozzi, and the Penrose and Keiller Dada and Surrealist bequests. The use of motifs inspired by the London house of Sir John Soane added a further layer of complexity. The effect is triumphantly ahistorical: in true Surrealist fashion, it is as if a ghostly but tangible discourse is alive and reverberating within the building. Orchestrated to interpret and reflect upon this richly layered narrative, the gallery is designed as an active participant in the display of art rather than as a passive backdrop.

The Dean's very ordered plan was created to reflect an alternative view of art and architectural history. Rejecting the conventional 'white-box' gallery – a place of purity and tranquillity where

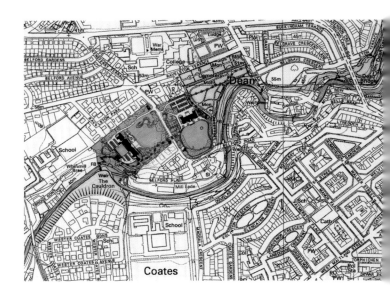

works of art are allowed to 'speak for themselves' – TFP devised a space characterised by richness and vibrancy. They created a tactile environment of puns and promises, providing visitors with points of reference that sharpen visual awareness.

Rather than emphasising the separation between the old and the new parts of the building, Farrell introduced what he calls an 'Emmenthal cheese effect' into the building's section. Spaces are burrowed through and hollowed out; there is no

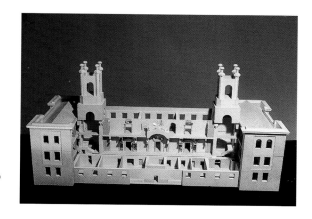

consistency of size or ceiling height; rooms are subjected to a variety of colour and lighting effects; and circulation spaces, as well as exhibition spaces, are all about sensory experience.

This is suggestive architecture that draws on its powers to move and intrigue the visitor; it does not reflect an agenda that seeks to be rational or modernist. The dominant trend in contemporary architecture is for architects to accentuate their new insertions by using high-tech materials that override the building's existing details. The idea behind the Dean Gallery is for the new architecture to be barely perceived, appearing to be part of the original building's own process of accretion.

Hamilton's Orphanage is peppered with

oddities, the most apparent of which is the conflicting vocabulary of styles on the entrance elevation (austerity of Greek Revival combined with the frivolity of Baroque). The palatial scale of the exterior must have meant little to the orphaned children, while the inside of the building offered little in the way of rewarding sensory experience. Ocular openings above fireplaces meant that the children could be watched at all times; boys and girls had separate wings, divided by thick walls, a central passageway and double doors; and only the sick room had windows with views.

Although Hamilton is generally portrayed as the rational nineteenth-century architect, the construction of the Dean Orphanage was full of contradic-

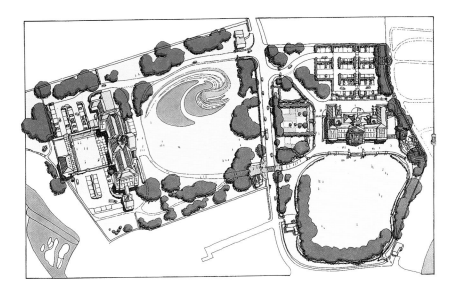

The masterplan incorporates the Dean Gallery, the SNGMA and the grounds in between.

▼

Long section showing the new vertical and horizontal connectivity.

A Two light-chimneys run from new skylights down through the floors, culminate in a sunken sculpture cavity and flood the ground- and first-floor corridor vistas with natural light.

B Existing chimney towers house staircases and signal the building's main circulation route.

C Dormer windows are positioned in the valley between the main roofs and connect down through the setpiece entrances to the first-floor galleries. A circular floor light, containing trapped pieces of sculpture, illuminates the entrances to the ground-floor galleries. Vitrines on either side of the floor lights cut into the floor to illuminate the basement corridor.

D The central entrance portico connects the ground and first floor, giving further transparency and connectedness to the previously closed-off and compartmentalised building.

tions and odd juxtapositions. In the quest to bring the building back to life as a gallery for Surrealist works of art, TFP were happy to exploit this theme.

Farrell's primary task was to resuscitate the inside of the building, introducing the vibrancy of the exterior into the interior spaces. This is achieved by cross-breeding and juxtaposing the existing work of Thomas Hamilton with motifs inspired by the more joyful work of Sir John Soane's London house. In this way, remnants of orphanage life, such as surveillance windows (symbolising oppression) are reborn as Soanian *oculi* (objects of delight). Soane's presence reveals itself throughout the building, but especially in the constrained space of the entry-level corridor – a keyhole through which glimpses can be had of the organisational elements of the building. The corridor, painted deep blue, is central to the design both visually and atmospherically. Threading its way north–south along the Dean's central axis, it provides views into the two stair towers that lead to each wing, the gallery floor above – the ceiling is punctured with ocular floor lights – and to galleries, café and shop. The *oculi* device results in a dark/light space imbued with both mystery and joy, the roots of which are clearly with Soane.

The placing of miscellaneous objects in areas of the building other than the galleries reflects TFP's

▲

TFP added widened pavements (removing unsightly and dangerous parked cars) at Belford Road and a new road crossing, allowing pedestrians free and direct access from the Dean Gallery to the SNGMA. These link the two galleries physically and visually, emphasising the 'art campus' status of the connected landscape through new openings in the Dean's stone perimeter wall.

▼

Cross section.

wish to abandon the formal hierarchies that usually divide exhibition areas and public spaces. At the Dean, objects throughout the gallery act as springboards for the imagination. Discovering plaster casts dropped into corridor floorlights or curios displayed in vitrines, in niches and on the tops of lintels within the structured setting of an art gallery creates a surprise that alerts the viewer to the never-ending implications of looking – a theme that was also central to Surrealist thinking. As in Soane's London house, colour is used to delineate spatial parameters, to evoke certain moods by emphasising the effects of light, and to create a sense of delight in the viewer.

The Gallery is like a theatre in which each space is animated by a formal and/or symbolic event. Interventions range from the major to the subtle. The most spectacular feature of the Gallery is the hall, specially designed to exhibit Eduardo Paolozzi's 9-metre-high sculpture of the Roman god Vulcan. This unfamiliarly narrow but double-height gallery provides an uplifting, slightly surreal space for reflection away from the main galleries. Other interventions are subtle, such as the gift shop's display cases, which are inserted below floor level and provide small light wells for the basement.

Often, the most surprising elements of the Dean are those created by Hamilton and accentuated in the new design – such as the unusual occurrence of *oculi* placed above fireplaces in the space normally reserved for flues (it is possible to stand in front of the hearth and look into an adjoining room or lightwell) and the Baroque-style chimneys, placed in two clusters above the two stair towers.

Reflecting the work of Thomas Hamilton and Sir John Soane, the design of the Dean is based on a magpie approach – motifs from past and present are used to carve out an architectural discourse. The Gallery is multifaceted in design, and wider – both physically and metaphorically – than a contemporary 'white-box' gallery with clearly delineated boundaries. The Dean's design celebrates the heritage that flows through it, imbues this with the exotic and emotional, and sculpts it into an architecture for everybody.

Sculpture and landscape have been inextricably intertwined to provide a complex variety of routes which will change with the seasons and the addition and relocation of the pieces. The buildings and the landscape are enhanced by the art works, either by their selection and juxtaposition, or by their having been commissioned for these particular sites.

DEAN GALLERY APPRAISAL
BY DORIS LOCKHART-SAATCHI

Courtesy of Blueprint

Terry Farrell's conversion of a former home for orphaned children in Edinburgh into an internationally important centre for Dada and Surrealist art and archives opened last year. One of several highly successful Scottish lottery projects, the Dean Gallery, as it is known, has met with only muted approval from Anglo-centric museum buffs south of the border. Yet Farrell has stitched together contributions from architectural idiosyncrats Thomas Hamilton and John Soane; Surrealist expert Roland Penrose; collector, former golf champion and Paolozzi patron Gabrielle Keiller; and artist visionaries William Blake and Eduardo Paolozzi into a brilliant patchwork where intention

◄

The landform as constructed, with ponds, terraces and paths set out to accord with the Hénon Attractor, a form relevant to the Chaos Theory inspiration for the three-dimensional land sculpture.

▼

The level change introduced to provide a dramatic approach to the Dean Gallery from the north, expressed in a massive stone retaining wall, has been embellished by sculpture by Ian Hamilton Finlay which relates to the building, its context and previous use.

and accident have equal weight.

Farrell was commissioned for the £9 million project in 1994 after interviews with a shortlist of architects that included Rick Mather, John Miller, Piers Gough and John McAslan. Eccentric in the extreme, the building is one of four so called 'pauper palaces' on high ground to the west of the city by the Water of Leith which were built in the mid-nineteenth century by prosperous Scots to signal their own elevated position and a dutiful concern for those less fortunate.

One of the 'palaces' is now the Scottish National Gallery of Modern Art. Standing a short distance away and at right angles to it, Hamilton's orphanage evolved in its new function as a member gallery of the National

Galleries of Scotland (NGS) network on the back of three coincidences. The first was the need to locate adequate storage facilities for the NGS's extensive collection. At around the same time, Eduardo Paolozzi donated his collection and the contents of his studio alongside important acquisitions of Surrealist art and archives from the Roland Penrose and Gabrielle Keiller estates. The third factor was the need to move the NGS headquarters.

Using the typology of the English country house, Hamilton designed his building to appear twice its size through the illusory device of the narrow 'H' block with projecting pavilions at each corner. Unassuming Tuscan columns, a Greek Revival portico, austere interiors and largely unembellished windows are in direct contrast to an ornate attic and Baroque-inspired towers that

the central section. The four main rooms within the latter are stacked on top of each other and joined vertically by the double-height hall, a suggestion, says Farrell, from NGS director Timothy Clifford, and by the stairs in the towers; and horizontally by reinstating a central corridor that forms a somewhat mysterious esplanade. The permanent collection, shop and café are in the 'fixed' rooms on the ground floor, while the more flexible upstairs spaces are designed for temporary exhibitions.

Soanian tricks abound. The pediments of the corridor openings are hinged to allow access for objects up to 1.5m wide. Lantern lights in the tower are inclined to bring in the maximum amount of light. Farrell has installed his own 'found' objects in niches and above lintels. Colour defines spaces and evokes mood-rich, murky blue in the corridor, sunny yellow on end walls and in the stairwells. At one end of the ground floor, a mirror reflects into eternity.

Everywhere Farrell plays on the original oddities in Hamilton's design which help determine its amazing suitability for its current use. One such oddity is the theme of surveillance evidenced by numerous occuli. Like Soane, Hamilton has placed them above fireplaces, a device to warm the hearts of all self respecting surrealists. Farrell has added two occuli in the first floor corridor. He has also appropriated Hamilton's obsession with chimneys that vented smoke to the outside for his own preoccupation with drawing light down through the chutes to illuminate the building's interior. He

▲

Visitors often think that the spectacular volumes of the transformed building were part of the original architecture, yet its plain interior contrasted with its exuberant exterior.

▶

One of the two *oculi*, situated between the ground and first floors, containing exhibits trapped between two sheets of glass.

◀

Paolozzi's sculpture of Vulcan stands in the double-height hall, beneath reliefs from Cleish Castle.

function as chimney stacks and stairwells, a stylistic contradiction befitting a house for Surrealism and one that Farrell made full use of in his redesign.

The first task that faced the architects was the development of a functional plan within the constraints of the building's Grade A listing. Farrell organised it around three key elements: the four corner pavilions, the twin stair towers and the central 'temple' front. His manoeuvres not only serve the purpose of the building but also heighten its original eccentricity.

The plan was divided into three tranches: the basement storage, the administration facilities in the wings and the public exhibition spaces in

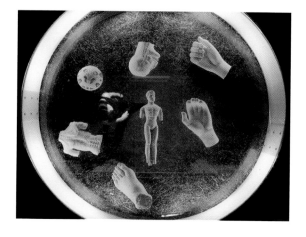

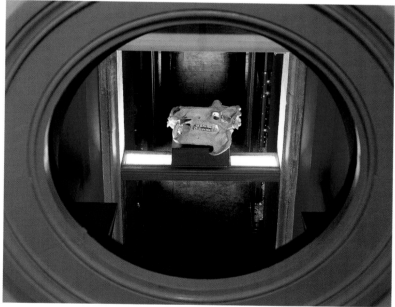

◂▴
Sequence showing ground-floor main axis corridor.

reinforces the Surrealist penchant for unsettling insights into a normally hidden world by cutting out the floor beneath two of the ground floor vitrines to light the basement and at the same time provide the observant with secret views of the space beneath their feet.

The best synthesis of the main strands of influence in the building can be found in the café. There the visitor encounters Hamilton's elegant Classicist ideas and Farrell's own admiration for Soane's taste for the juxtaposition of apparently unrelated objects. There also is the Surrealist-Dada-Pop alternative view of art and art history expressed by Paolozzi's sculpted figure of Newton taken from a drawing by Blake, who challenged Newton's rational view of man.

The tinted fibreglass sculpture is a new interpretation for the Dean Gallery of Paolozzi's 1989

The Gabrielle Keiller Library with its display of Dada and Surrealist manuscripts and publications.

View from the new café looking towards the Paolozzi Gallery on the ground floor. Paolozzi's sculpture of Newton is in the foreground.

CAFÉ

View into the café from the main ground-floor corridor looking through one of the vitrines to the sculpture placed on the café table.

Master of the Universe work and shows the scientist measuring the constellation Aries, the ram. As the animal signifying St Francis, the patron saint of orphans, the ram is depicted sculpturally in the entrance lobby by the original designers. Farrell's contributions to this leitmotif are the lights in the café ceiling arranged as the stars of the Aries constellation, and the design of the café chairs – an off-the-peg model given horns, cloven feet and brass studs marking the constellation on its seat. In defiance of the law of physics he discovered, Newton can be elevated from his position on the large central table for dinner parties.

'I've always been interested in the alternative' says Farrell, 'not just to be different, but because it's interesting to flip the coin and see what's on the other side.' Farrell's M 16 and Charing Cross buildings were very much out of sync with the prevailing modernist orthodoxy of the Eighties. Though they were dismissed recently by a critic as 'archi-tainment' they have become landmarks even winning a grudging affection from some. It is always possible that flipping the coin can result in innovation rather than just novelty. The site and design of the Millennium Dome have drawn attention to and admiration for Farrell's Blackwall

▲
The north elevation provides
the view from the car park
entrance. The large sculpture
of Vulcan can be seen
through the window.

Tunnel ventilation ducts, designed in 1961 as one
of his first projects. Not only are they beautiful
forms, but they represent a technological first in
Britain, the use of sprayed concrete on metal
frames to create stable, free form shapes.

The experience of Farrell's Dean Gallery is one
of total immersion, especially upon entering the
ground floor corridor where high ceilings, darkly
coloured lights and a multitude of objects apparently afloat in glass vitrines suggest a mysterious
journey through the unfamiliar, a sensation not
unlike being underwater.

In 1985 Paolozzi wrote that an ideal museum
would be 'in an old building – perfectly abandoned
where there would be a sensation from the history
of things, not only superb originals but fakes,
combined with distinguished 'reproductions',

copies of masterpieces both in painting and
engineering'. Paolozzi's statement could be an
excerpt from a manifesto for the Surrealist and
Dada art movements that have influenced him so
heavily. It also reads, in retrospective, like a brief
for Farrell, whose integrated celebration of Blake's
vision and Newtonian reason has created one of
the best museum buildings in the country.

The Mound

The Mound

◀

Aerial view showing the Mound as it exists. William Playfair's two great galleries – the Royal Scottish Academy (left) and the National Gallery of Scotland – form a bridge between the Old and New Towns. The railway arch penetrates beneath.

▶

Historical drawing showing the landfill from the New Town which formed the bridge on which Playfair's two galleries would be built.

▶

TFP's 1993 design for the National Gallery of Scottish Art and History in Glasgow's Kelvingrove, which formed part of a study for the future of the National Galleries of Scotland's collection (see pp.83–88). The site was abandoned in favour of expanding existing galleries in Edinburgh, and TFP's Mound scheme carries on from its involvement in this project.

▼

Plans.

The Mound is at the heart of Edinburgh's history and its urban story. James Craig, architect of the New Town, saw this 'land bridge' – constructed from the rubble used to make the New Town between 1781 and 1830 – as a temporary structure, while William Playfair built two buildings on it: the Royal Institution, later reincarnated as the National Gallery of Scotland, and the Royal Scottish Academy. He also designed the Edinburgh railway, which runs below the Mound. The tension and balance of the landscaped valley (the former Nor' Loch), interrupted by a land bridge between the Old and New Towns, is the key to the Mound's urban drama. Playfair's placing of two buildings as points in space – the National Gallery of Scotland and the Royal Scottish Academy – celebrates the valley as a continuous expanse and

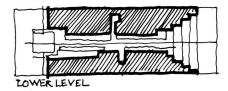

LOWER LEVEL

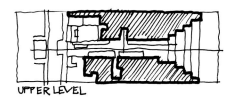

UPPER LEVEL

MOUND LEVEL

▶

Sketches showing stages of the Mound's development as part of TFP's proposals:

1 Land bridge built to connect New Town and Old Town across the valley.
2 Bridge with the Royal Scottish Academy and the National Gallery of Scotland – two major public buildings by Playfair built on the Mound to create an arts acropolis.
3 The railway travels along the bottom of the valley gardens to Waverley Station, perforating the land bridge.
4 Proposed connections link both sides of the valley gardens and the RSA and NGS below ground.

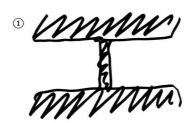
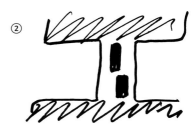
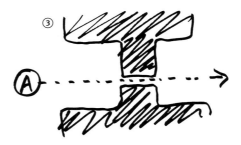
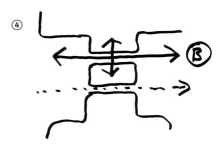

▶

Engineer's drawing illustrating the proposed construction.

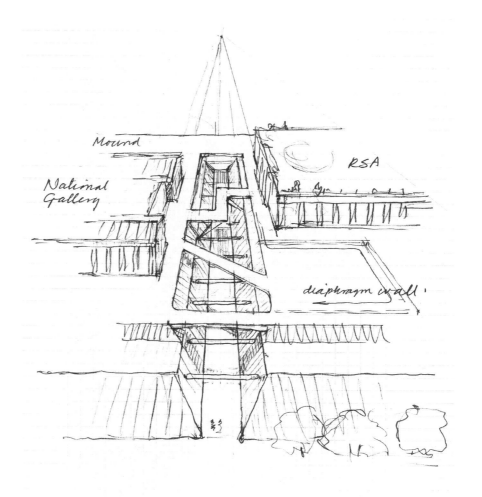

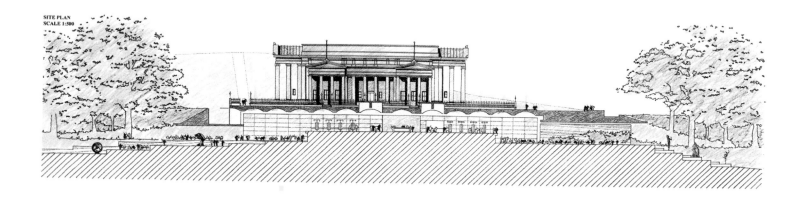

SITE PLAN
SCALE 1:500

▲
Cross-section proposal for
the two gardens.

▼
Plan of the Mound's lower
level. Connections are made
between the gardens to the
east and west and the
galleries to the north and
south. A shop sits in the
centre.

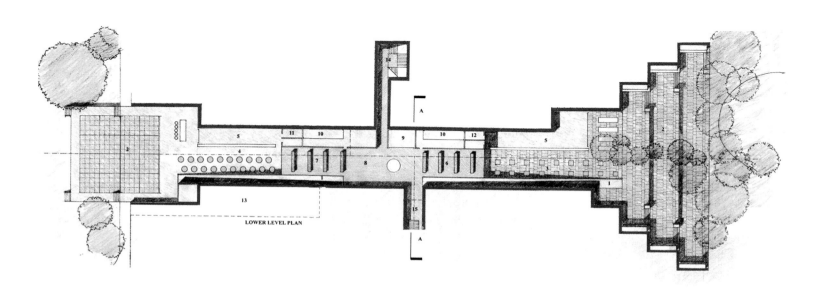

LOWER LEVEL PLAN

▶

Concept drawings by Terry
Farrell.

▲

1:500 model showing
connection to gardens with
galleries above.

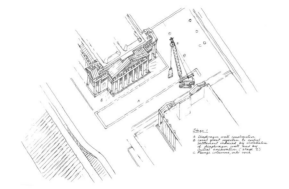
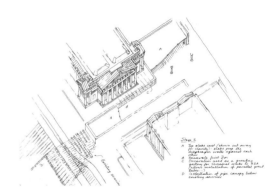

▲

Aerial view of model.

▼

Construction drawings
showing the engineering of
the slot between the NGS
and the RSA.

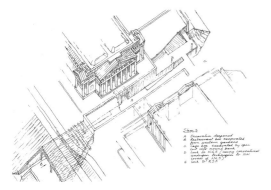

acknowledges the power of landscape, rather than urban or architectural links, to connect the Old and New Towns.

TFP's competition entry focused on a celebration of connectedness, in the style of the Mound itself. The National Galleries of Scotland's brief was for a building that would act as a catalyst to revitalise the Royal Scottish Academy and the National Gallery of Scotland. TFP were asked to provide a façade-less solution that would not compete with Playfair's Neoclassical setpiece at high level. The solution was an underground grotto, or undercroft, linking East and West Princes Street Gardens through a sequence of inspirational spaces, which also forms a strong directional axis on either side of the Mound. The grotto has the same crowd-pulling effect that the new railway, running under the Mound, had for nineteenth-century visitors.

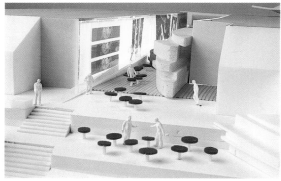

Illuminated by natural light from a glazed roof, the grotto provides a shared entrance to the National Gallery of Scotland and the Royal Scottish Academy, along with a ticket office and cloakrooms. Gallery shops occupy underground spaces. A backlit wall 60 metres by 4.5 metres is used as a display area for prints and photographs, and for video and film projection. This central section is linked with the entrance space above by transparent sculpture plinths that act as light wells. Sloping public walkways lead down to the gardens at either end, providing bright, daylit spaces for the building's interior. The east end's café and the west end's restaurant engage with existing and re-routed footpaths on the Mound. The largest spaces are the lecture theatre and education suite, located in the south-eastern corner of the Royal Scottish Academy.

Ocean Point

Ocean Point

The paired buildings operate as a similar-yet-different asymmetric entity, with views and light being sufficiently varied for each building to promote its own character.

The design of the Ocean Point development has evolved from a brief requiring approximately 200,000 square feet of lettable office accommodation split into two buildings and located in the emerging business quarter at the Port of Leith, Edinburgh's historic dockland.

These buildings enjoy a formal relationship with Terence Conran's masterplan (in particular, the Ocean Terminal building, the key component of the area's retail sector designed to increase the Port's berth capacity and be a permanent site for the former Royal Yacht *Britannia*) and balance the residential and commercial developments both under way and anticipated in future stages.

The site is located on one of a series of spaces connected by several routes leading from the traditional core of Leith to the new amenities being developed. This space is embraced by the two buildings, and is accessed either between them or

▲
The Ocean Point development is set within a colossal redevelopment initiative encompassing the entire water's edge of the Port of Leith, involving massive new infrastructure and land reclamation.

▼
Responding to the linear blocks of Ocean Terminal and the Scottish Executive building, Ocean Point establishes a vertical landmark within Conran's masterplan.

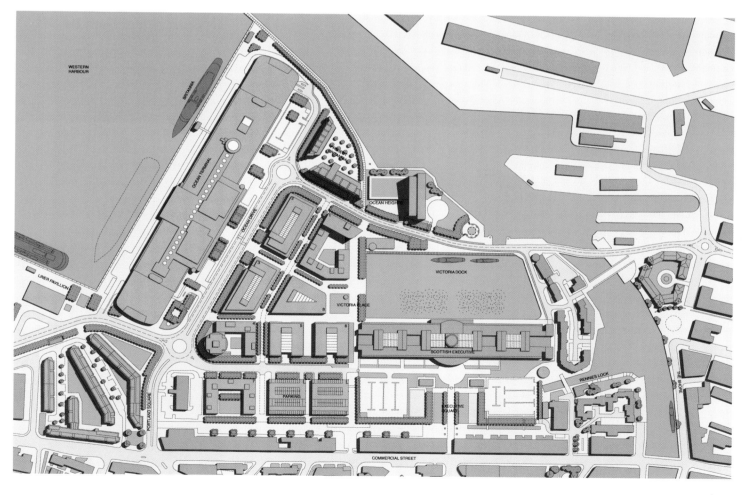

◄

Computer-generated view of the south-west corner.

►

Landscape structure sketch. As well as accommodating seating, shelter is provided with an elevated view of the port.

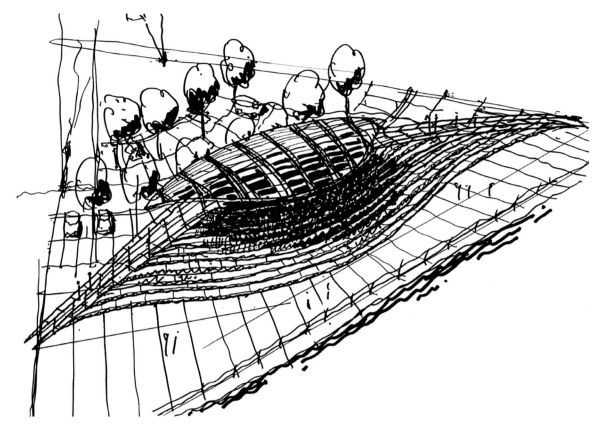

▼

The arrangement of the landscape treatment between the buildings – including planting, car park and giant sculptural form – connects the individual elements of the development as a geometrically integrated whole.

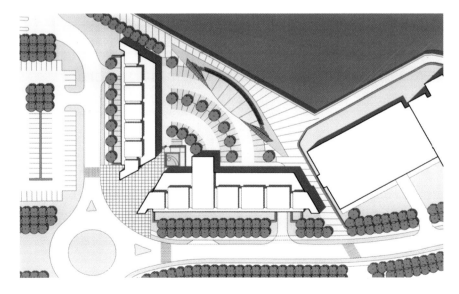

off the public walkway extruding along the edge of the sea wall towards Ocean Terminal. Animation of the space by office workers, pedestrians and visitors to other local amenities is accommodated by the siting of a large canopied sculpture incorporating an elevated view of the working dock and the historic heart of the Port of Leith, providing an appropriate waterside frontage for the development.

The buildings relate firmly to the geometries set out in the masterplan and have clean lines relating to nautical themes. Carefully detailed glass and metal panels reflect the sea, sky and panorama of the city in glittering clarity, providing unique views in all directions in what will become the pioneering core of the emerging revived settlement.

The silhouette and building edges have been sculpted into distinct profiles to act as a foil to the purity of the sweep of the principal facades, each of which, facing a different point of the compass, will allow light to reflect and pass through to differing degrees, dependent on the time of day and season, giving a dynamic, ever-changing appearance.

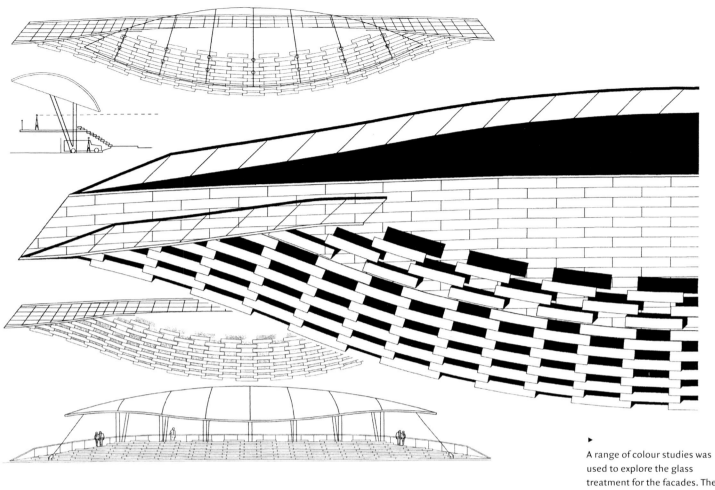

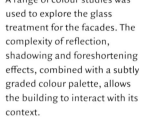

A range of colour studies was used to explore the glass treatment for the facades. The complexity of reflection, shadowing and foreshortening effects, combined with a subtly graded colour palette, allows the building to interact with its context.

▲
Landscape structure sketch showing details of the seating.

▼
The distinctive profile of each floor plate accommodates the site's angular geometry and promotes efficient office use.

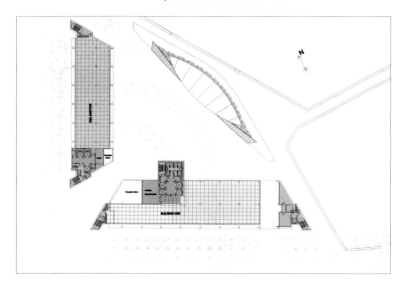

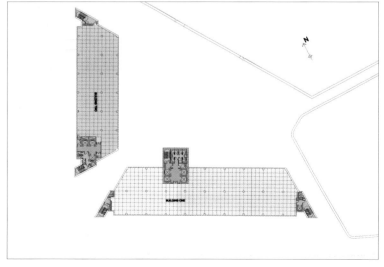

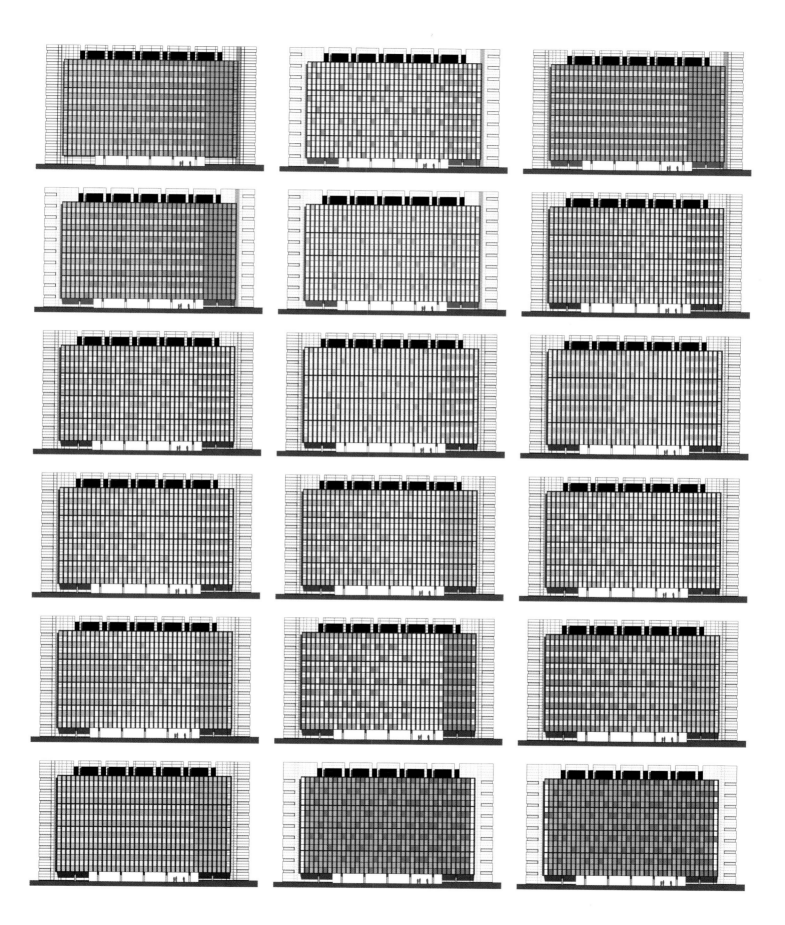

▲

Early computer drawing. A pair of slim, glass-clad towers have been designed as a response to the waterside setting and the linear, gridded nature of the immediate development, which includes the Scottish Executive building and Ocean Terminal.

▲

Night-time view. The scale of development throughout the port allows for a variety of integrated uses, resulting in a district of distinct identity.

▶

Early sketch indicating the two framed slabs of glass with edges emphasised by embracing towers.

South-East Wedge

South-East Wedge

◄
Aerial photograph of the South-East Wedge development area, comprising a former colliery site, small diffuse existing communities and agricultural land.

▶
A number of discrete and integrated settlements are proposed to form a balance of new communities and workplaces in a sustainable matrix.

▶
The new town of Shawfair provides 3,500 homes, green spaces accommodating pedestrian and cycle routes connecting the town with the countryside and a mixed-use town centre with a central rail halt.

The South-East Wedge proposes to be the most significant comprehensively planned community settlement in Lothian for decades, and will contain vibrant, self-contained communities in attractive settings. The development will follow a sustainable pattern, with an emphasis on good community facilities and public transport links within the settlement and with other local amenities. New buildings will be of a high quality and contribute towards a robust and sympathetic urban design framework, designed to accord with the character of the landscape and appropriate existing communities.

In developing the proposals contained within the Local Plan documents for the City of Edinburgh and Midlothian Councils, the aspirations for coordinated public transport links, continuity of Green Belt space and a pattern of sustainable development have evolved in accordance with the established principles. These take into account environmental, geological and mining surveys

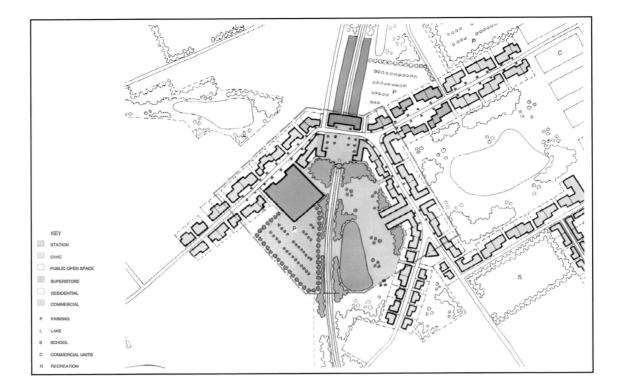

▶
Town centre plan. The existing road network has been retained to permit the growth of the town to take place organically, but with access to residential areas separated from business uses.

KEY

☐ STATION
☐ CIVIC
☐ PUBLIC OPEN SPACE
☐ SUPERSTORE
☐ RESIDENTIAL
☐ COMMERCIAL

P   PARKING
L   LAKE
S   SCHOOL
C   COMMERCIAL UNITS
R   RECREATION

which have clarified the suitability for development of all study areas.

Three locations for major housing developments and associated community facilities are proposed in Shawfair and North and South Danderhall. Two new primary school facilities are to be provided in Shawfair, linked to a new town centre, and existing school facilities in Danderhall are to be improved and extended.

Business development is planned at Whitehill Mains and Todhills, with land allocated for economic development as well as being promoted at the former Monktonhall Colliery site and adjacent to Millerhill Marshalling Yards.

The new development is to be served by an extensive coordinated transport network, containing cycle routes, and bus and rail connections at the core of the new community, specifically planned with a rail halt at its core.

The distinctive character of the existing landscape – enjoying views of Arthur's Seat, the Pentland Hills and the Bass Rock from its ridges –

▶
Site analysis studies showing the relationship between the existing landscape and the proposed built form.

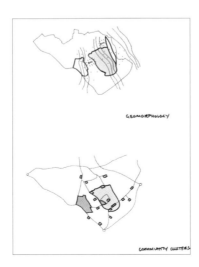

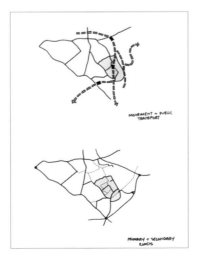

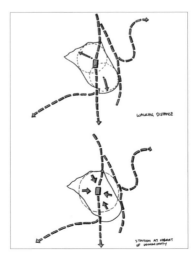

A number of precedent study sketches analysed the nature of the built form in and around the South-East Wedge in order to discover – and recreate, where appropriate – the *genius loci* for the new settlements.

will be exploited constructively to form groups of settlements developed in accordance with the existing nature of the Green Belt, as well as providing a continuity of green space – amenity, recreational and ambient – within the urban forms.

Approximately 20% of the new homes will constitute social housing (both shared ownership and rented houses) and these are to be distributed evenly throughout the development, so that balanced communities may be achieved.

The core settlement at the heart of the South-East Wedge is the new Shawfair development. A centrally located rail halt will be established early in the implementation of the new community, to provide access from Shawfair (and via its associated park-and-ride facilities, other local centres) to the City of Edinburgh, and rail links will eventually be formed to Penicuik and south to the Borders. A mixed-used town centre will have at its core a new open urban space, with the rail line running beneath, fringed by civic, retail and higher-density

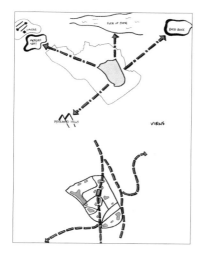

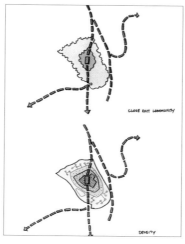

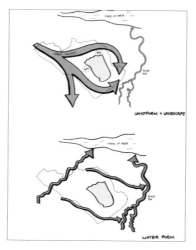

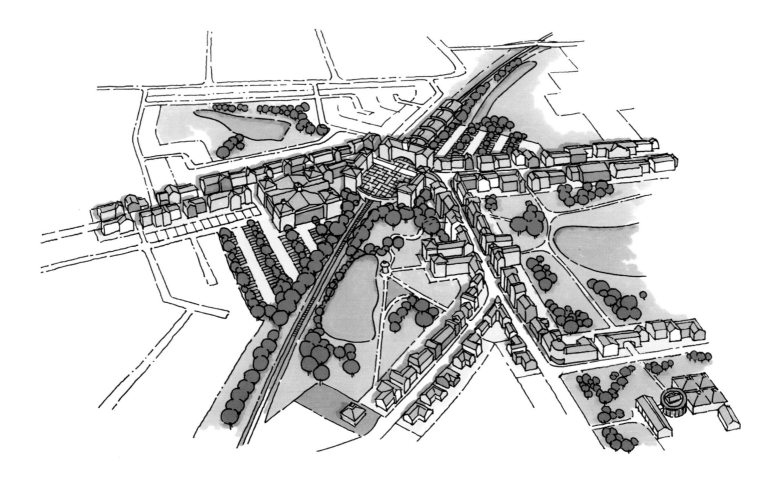

Town centre aerial view. New buildings have been arranged along existing landscape and topographical features so as to engage naturally. Green space and recreation facilities have been allowed to penetrate the centre of the settlement, with the scale of buildings gradually increasing to form a civic core, asserting a positive identity.

housing uses. A supermarket and linked green spaces (which provide for sustainable urban drainage features as well as allowing pedestrian and cycle links to permeate the development) ensure a variety of built form and amenity. Building heights of two or two-and-a-half storeys will be prevalent in the centre, rising up to three and four storeys in the town centre and around the new public space in order to provide local clusters of higher density or points of vertical focus to assist in place-making and promoting reference features to give the settlement its own particular character.

Towards the perimeter of Shawfair (still generally within a five-minute walk of the rail halt, and a couple of minutes at most from a bus stop) housing densities drop. Green fingers of space are permitted

to infiltrate at the edges, reinforcing the Green Belt continuity, links to recreational facilities, and allowing the natural ridges to be expressed without compromising their integrity.

The South-East Wedge represents an innovative yet sustainable development, embodying principles that promote environment, community and balance between a new urban settlement and its landscape context, as a part of the character of this part of Lothian.

Braehead Retail Complex

Braehead Retail Complex

This scheme comprised a 600,000 square foot shopping centre and 150,000 square feet of leisure and restaurant space, a business park, a retail warehouse and a hotel. A masterplan approach was adopted to unify the site and to create an identity for a neglected and derelict location. A framework or grid layout with key locations identified by bold colours and forms orientates and directs the shopper around the site. The planning of the shopping centre itself is on the traditional dumb-bell principle, with clear visual links between anchor stores, and food court, restaurant and leisure facilities located at an equal distance between them. Entrances are strategically located to promote pedestrian circulation through the complex, and car parking is evenly distributed around the building, well-screened behind avenues of mature trees.

The approach to the landscape is based on contrasts between abstract shapes and natural forms so that familiar elements become surprising, thus introducing an element of fantasy.

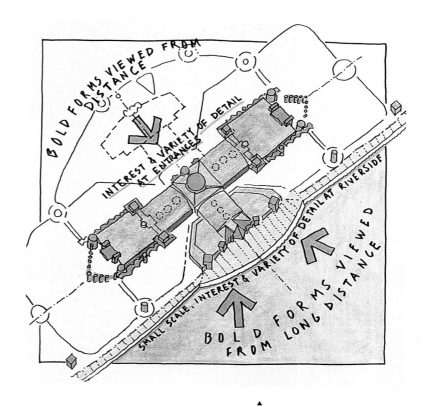

▲
Concept sketch: views.

▼
Concept sketch: add-on elements.

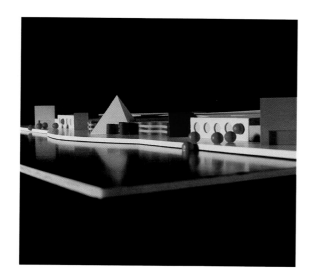

◄
Study model: store and entrance gateways.

▲
Study model: perspective view of leisure element along the river frontage.

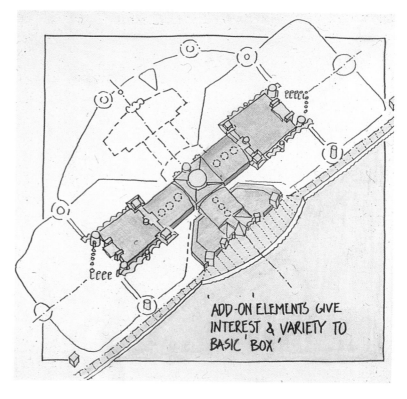

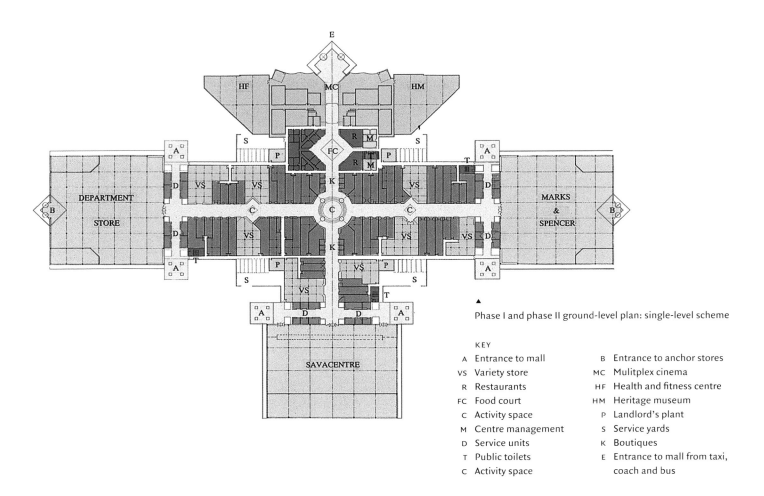

▲

Phase I and phase II ground-level plan: single-level scheme

KEY

A	Entrance to mall	B	Entrance to anchor stores
VS	Variety store	MC	Mulitplex cinema
R	Restaurants	HF	Health and fitness centre
FC	Food court	HM	Heritage museum
C	Activity space	P	Landlord's plant
M	Centre management	S	Service yards
D	Service units	K	Boutiques
T	Public toilets	E	Entrance to mall from taxi, coach and bus
C	Activity space		

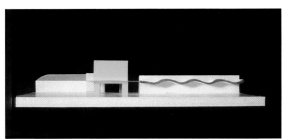

▲

Eye-level study of entrance to major stores.

◄

Study model: building two.

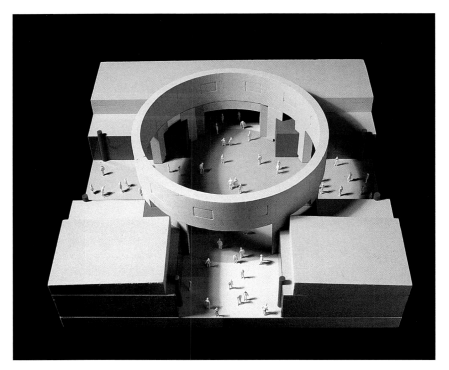

National Gallery
of Scottish Art and History

National Gallery
of Scottish Art and History

In February 1993 Terry Farrell was invited by the Glasgow Development Agency to put forward a vision for the new National Gallery of Scottish Art and History in Kelvingrove Park that would reflect the vigour, variety and invention of Scottish art and culture. The Gallery was to embrace the evolving tradition of Scottish art from its beginnings to the present day. Changing exhibitions and a complete library of the history of Scottish art would create an environment in which the general public and scholars alike could appreciate and study Scotland's national heritage.

The proposals for the Gallery, in harmony with the park landscape, Kelvingrove Art Gallery and Museum and the University of Glasgow, would revive the historic role of the park as Glasgow's major site for arts festivals and other major cultural events.

Although funding for a single new large gallery in Glasgow was ultimately not available and the project was not to proceed in this form, Terry Farrell's work on the Kelvingrove proposal – and the need for additional accommodation for the National Galleries of Scotland – was to culminate in the Dean Gallery and Masterplan commission.

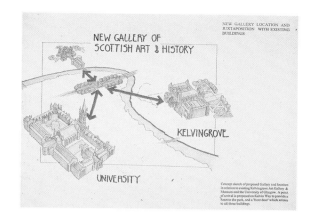

Concept sketch of proposed Gallery and location in relation to existing Kelvingrove Art Gallery and Museum and the University of Glasgow. A point of arrival is proposed in Kelvin Way to provide a heart to the park, and a 'front door' which relates to all three buidings.

Detail of model.

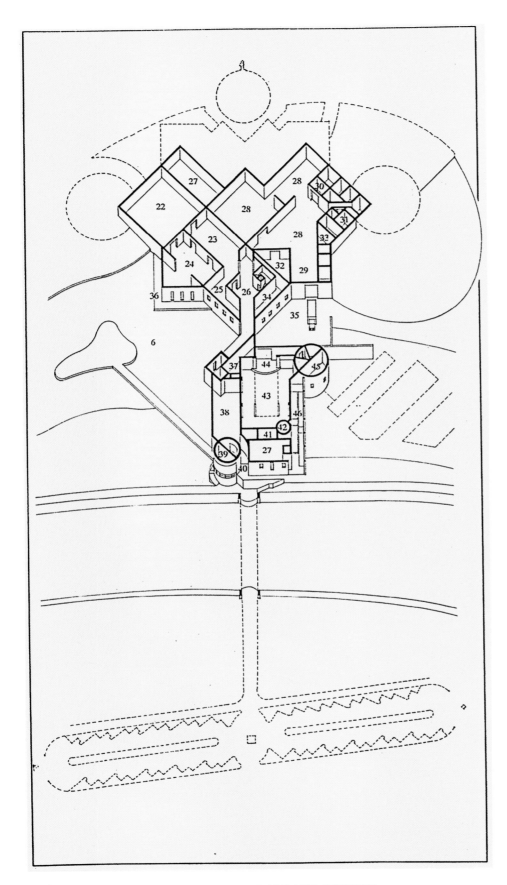

▶

Upper ground floor

◀

Lower ground floor

KEY

1 Car park
2 New bridge
3 River Kelvin
4 Entrance building
5 Gallery building
6 Lake
7 Stewart Memorial Fountain
8 Galleries
9 Sculpture galleries
10 Sculpture terraces
11 Entrance
12 Art lift
13 Boardroom
14 Restaurant
15 Artist's studio
16 Female toilets
17 Male toilets
18 Education rooms
19 Shop
20 Entry and orientation area
21 Ramp from car-park level
22 Library
23 Drawings and prints
24 Reference
25 Photographic archive
26 Display for prints, drawings and photographs
27 Plant
28 Reserve galleries
29 Handling area
30 Art lift
31 Conservation workshop and studio
32 Handling workshop
33 Conservation offices
34 Warders' accommodation
35 Loading bay
36 Lakeside terrace
37 Kitchen
38 Curatorial accommodation
39 Artist's studio
40 Staff entrance
41 Toilets
42 Reception and cloakroom
43 Lecture theatre
44 Backstage / changing / projection
45 Seminar room
46 Ramp to gallery level
47 Sculpture galleries
48 Sculpture terraces
49 Stewart Memorial Fountain
50 Car parking

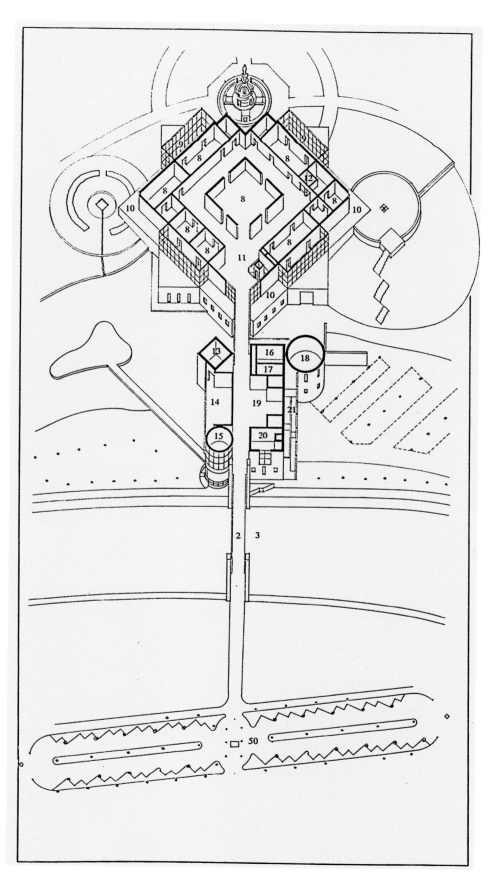

►
Axonometric of galleries.

KEY
A Temporary exhibition gallery
B Permanent narrative gallery
C Permanent branch galleries
D Sculpture conservatory
E Sculpture terrace

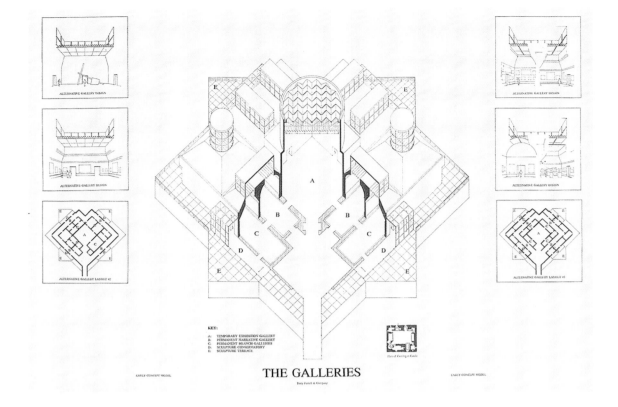

THE GALLERIES

◄
Model: detail of gallery,
illuminated.

►
Model.

Model: aerial view.

Appendices

Appendix 1: List of Works 1992–2002

† Unbuilt scheme
‡ Current project

1984–92
South Bank Arts Centre masterplan,
London Borough of Lambeth †

1987–92
Alban Gate, Lee House, 125 London Wall,
London EC2

1988–92
Vauxhall Cross, Government Headquarters
Building (MI6), Albert Embankment,
London SE1

1989–92
Paternoster Square masterplan,
City of London, EC2 †
AIA Award for Urban Design, 1994

1989–92
Mixed-use masterplan, Quarry Hill, Leeds

1989–92
Chiswick Business Park, London Borough
of Hounslow †

1989–95
Edinburgh International Conference Centre,
Morrison Street, Financial District
*Silver Medal, Edinburgh Architectural
Association Design Award 1995*
Civic Trust Award 1996
RIBA Award 1996

1990–92
Brindleyplace masterplan, Birmingham

1990–2001
Exchange Financial District masterplan

1990–
South Kensington Station and mixed-use
development, London SW1 ‡

1991
Medical Centre, South Birmingham
Report on the development of Heathrow
Airport for the British Airports Authority
Commonwealth Trust Offices and Club,
London WC1 †
Spitalfields Market masterplan, London E1 †
Westminster Hospital redevelopment,
Horseferry Road, London SW1
Lloyds Bank headquarters, Pall Mall, London
WC2 †

1991–92
Lloyds Bank redevelopment, Lombard Street,
EC1 †
Mixed-use renovation and redevelopment
scheme, Grey Street, Newcastle

1991–93
Thameslink 2000 masterplan, Blackfriars,
London †

▲ **1991–95**
The Peak Tower, Hong Kong

▼ **1991–98**
Newcastle Quayside, Newcastle
Urban Design Award, Civic Trust 1998
*Lord Mayor's Design Award, Landscape &
Accessibility Category (Commendation) 1998*
RTPI Spaces Award 1998
Civic Trust Urban Design Award 1998
BURA Best Practice Award 1999

1991–98
Railway development, Farringdon Station,
London EC1 †

▲ **1991–**
Marsham Street Towers redevelopment (Home
Office HQ), London SW1 ‡

1992
Canon's Marsh, Bristol
Lisbon Expo masterplan, Lisbon waterfront †
Fort Canning Radio Tower, Singapore †

1992–94
Sainsbury's Supermarket, Harlow, Essex
Civic Trust Award 1994
RIBA Award 1995
Commendation, Civic Trust Award 1996

1992–95
Player's Theatre, Embankment Place, Villiers
Street, London WC2

▼ **1992–96**
British Consulate-General and British Council
Headquarters, Hong Kong

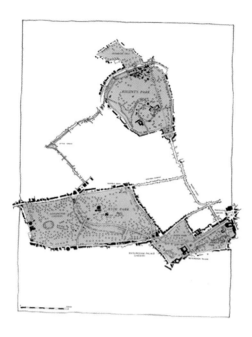

National Gallery of Scottish Art and History, Kelvingrove Park, Glasgow †

Hungerford Bridge redevelopment, London †

EFFRA site, Vauxhall, London SW8†

1992–96

▲ Royal Parks study, Royal Parks Review Group, London

1992–98

▾ Kowloon Station, Hong Kong

Masterplan for transport interchange with associated buildings

Best International Interchange Award, Integrated Transport Awards 2001

1993

Albertopolis outline proposal, London SW1 †

Ampang Tower, Kuala Lumpur †

Braehead retail complex, Glasgow †

Blackfriars Bridge, London †

SmithKline Beecham headquarters complex, Great Burgh, Epsom, Surrey †

1993–95

▲ Kowloon Ventilation Building, Hong Kong

▾ Barreiro Ferry Terminal and Station Development, Lisbon

National Heritage Library and Cultural Centre, Dubai †

Vasteras Railway Station, Vasteras, Sweden †

1993–96

▾ Do Rossio Station redevelopment, Lisbon

1993–2007

London Bridge Station redevelopment, London ‡

1994

Gare Do Oriente masterplan, Lisbon †

Sincere Insurance building, Hong Kong

Nathan Road tower, Hong Kong †

Shekou masterplan, Shenzen †

'Chester in Concert' performance space, Chester †

1994–95

Queen's Road masterplan, Hong Kong †

1994–

Keele University masterplan †

1994–98

Ebbsfleet masterplan, Kent †

1994–

▲ Port of Lisbon masterplan, Lisbon waterfront

1995

Subic Bay Freeport Central Area masterplan, Philippines †

Glasgow Business School, University of Glasgow †

Kennedy Town railway station, Hong Kong †

Cambourne masterplan, South Cambridgeshire

'C' Restaurant building, Seoul †

Landmark Tower, Kowloon

Landmark building, Northumberland Cross, Northumberland †

1995–96

Imperial Wharf redevelopment, London

1995–99

▲ 'Y' Headquarters building, Seoul †

▼ 'H' retail gallery and clinic building for arts centre masterplan, Seoul †

1995–

West Rail, Hong Kong

Station scheme design and masterplanning of West Kowloon Passenger Terminal, Kam Tin, Lok Ma Chau, Tseun Wan West, Yen Chow Street and Mei Foo stations

1996

High-speed railway station, Pusan, Korea †

Mixed-use redevelopment masterplan of historic centre, Castlegate, York †

Star Ferry Terminal redevelopment, Hong Kong †

Feasibility study to find new venue for English National Opera Lyric Theatre

▲ Samsung European Headquarters and masterplan, Boston Manor Park, London †

University of East London masterplan †

1996–99

Dean Centre Art Gallery and Masterplan, Edinburgh

Scottish Museum Award (Highly Commended) 1999

Sheraton Hotel Health Club and Spa, Exchange Financial District, Edinburgh

1996–2000

Bluewater Valley masterplan, Kent

▲ International Centre for Life, Newcastle

Landmark Millennium Project housing a new public square and a series of buildings with facilities to explore genetic science

Celebrating Construction Achievement Award (North-East), 2000

Copper in Architecture Awards (Commendation) 2000

1996–2001

▲ Transportation Centre for the Inchon International Airport, Seoul

▼ 1996–2003

Paddington Basin masterplan, London W2 ‡

1996–2005

London Bridge Station ‡

1996–

▼ Chelsea Creek (Lots Road Power Station), Chelsea, London ‡

▲ Three Quays Hotel/Tower Environs masterplan, Tower of London, SE1 ‡

1996–
Station improvement programme, Hong Kong

1997
Bucklersbury House office and retail development, London EC4 †

Computer Laboratory, University of Cambridge †

MTV European headquarters air-rights development, London NW1 †

Hungerford Bridge competition scheme, London †

Shandong International Conference and Exhibition Centre, Qingdao, China

1997–2001
▼ Crescent Housing, Newcastle ‡

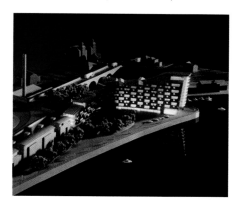

1997–2002
Blue Circle Cement Works, Kent ‡

1997–
▼ New National Aquarium, Silvertown, London ‡

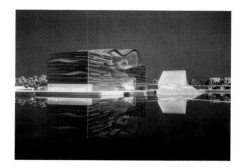

1998
Ferensway masterplan, Hull

Capability Green business park, Luton †

Carlton TV Headquarters, London W1 †

Chelsea Barracks, London

Residential scheme for existing barracks and rehousing of barracks to new site in New Covent Garden Market

Gresham Street redevelopment, London

Island Wharf, Hull

Liverpool Vision masterplan †

Maritime Square, Singapore

Waterfront masterplan and architecture †

Restoration and development of 15–17 Charlotte Square, Edinburgh

Piccadilly Gardens, Manchester †

Architect's Studio, 7 Hatton Street, London NW8

Springhead masterplan, Ebbsfleet, Thames Gateway †

1998–
Punggol Station, Singapore ‡

British University masterplan, Cairo †

1998–2000
▲ Beijing National Opera, Tiananmen Square, Beijing †

Westferry Circus Office development, Canary Wharf, London E14 ‡

Elephant & Castle masterplan, London SE1 †

1998–2001
Greenwich Promenade, London SE10 ‡

▲ The Deep Submarium, Sammy's Point, Hull
Millennium project housing a world-class aquarium exhibit, business and research centre

1998–
Euston Station redevelopment, London ‡

1999
Bermondsey Square masterplan, London †

Borough Road masterplan, London †

Courtyard development, Fitzwilliam Museum, Cambridge †

The Mound, Edinburgh

Undercroft linking National Galleries of Scotland with Royal Scottish Academy †

Ouseburn Village masterplan, Newcastle

▼ River Hull Corridor masterplan †

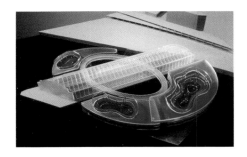

▲ Pacific North-West Aquarium and masterplan, Seattle ‡

Business community and mixed urban development, Stonecastle, Kent

Masterplan for disused colliery site, Westoe Hill, South Shields

World Squares masterplan, London

Royal Institution of Great Britain redevelopment, Albemarle Street, London W1 ‡

1999–2001
Waterfront regeneration, Margate

Campbell Park masterplan, Milton Keynes

1999–2000
Bank One headquarters, Cardiff †

2000–
Southern Gateway, South central Manchester ‡

Mixed-use development in new urban quarter

Nursery, Manchester Southern Gateway

▼ Macintosh Mill redevelopment, Manchester Southern Gateway

Bluewater Valley masterplan, Kent ‡

Brunswick Square redevelopment, Leeds

Clyde Corridor masterplan, Glasgow ‡

Guangzhou Daily Cultural Plaza, Guangzhou, China. Headquarters building †

Paradise Street redevelopment, Liverpool

Ocean Point, Edinburgh ‡

Commercial building

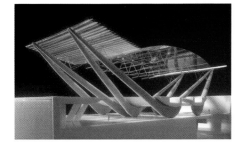

▲ Parramatta Rail Link, Sydney ‡

▼ Pearl Island masterplan, Shenzen ‡

Royal Docks masterplan, London †

▲ Swiss Cottage redevelopment, London NW3 ‡

Victoria & Albert Museum masterplan, London SW1 †

South Seattle masterplan, Seattle ‡

2001
▲ The Point, Paddington, London ‡

Headquarters building for Orange Communications

▼ Greenwich Peninsula masterplan, London ‡

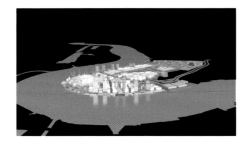

Bristol Brewery masterplan ‡

Petersham Housing, Richmond, London ‡

South-East Wedge masterplan, Edinburgh ‡

2002
▼ Buckingham Palace Redesigned ‡

London Clinic ‡

London Zoo masterplan ‡

Newcastle Central masterplan ‡

Newcastle University masterplan ‡

Preston masterplan ‡

Shoreditch Park masterplan ‡

Appendix 2: Terry Farrell & Partners

▲ Sir Terry Farrell

▲ Edinburgh Office staff, past and present

David Abdo

Sandy Anderson

Dominique Andrews

Simon Baker

Chris Barber

Michael Barry

Dorothy Batchelor

David Beynon

Nigel Bidwell

Nick Birchall

Jeremy Boole

Andy Bow

Toby Bridge

Andrew Burridge

John Campbell

Brian Chantler

Barrie Cheng

Mark Coles

Richard Davies

Neil de Prez

Dennis Dornan

Tom Edwards

Graham Fairley

Sue Farrell

Terry Farrell

Mark Floate

Nick Forbes

Jo Harrop

Moz Hussain

Karl James

Lily Jencks

Maggie Jones

Doris Lam

John Letherland

Donal Murphy

Asha Narbutt

Derek Nolan

Ike Ogbue

Dermot Patterson

Aidan Potter

Louise Potter

Sara Raybould

Tanni Rice

Peter Robinson

Earl Rutherford

Cherry Sherlock-Tanner

Mark Shirburne-Davies

Steve Smith

Philip Smithies

Jason Speechly-Dick

Alexandra Stevens

Doug Streeter

Paul Summerlin

Richard Tan

Kate Taylor

Mark Taylor

Ashok Tendle

Jane Tobin

Julian Tollast

Eugene Uys

Duncan Whatmore

Eiffel Wong

Chris Wood

Jes Worre

Karin Yiannakou

Gary Young

Nigel Young

▲ EDINBURGH OFFICE STAFF, 2002

Michael Barry

Dorothy Batchelor

David Davies

Neil de Prez

Chris Pyemont

Shahrazad Ujam

Duncan Whatmore

PICTURE CREDITS

All images courtesy of Terry Farrell & Partners unless stated. Front cover Keith Hunter; back cover (top) Richard Bryant / Arcaid; back cover (below) Tim Soar; page 2 Tim Soar; page 8 NRSC Ltd / Science Photo Library; page 14 bottom left Graeme Duncan; page 14 bottom right Nigel Young; page 15 Graeme Duncan; page 16 Keith Hunter; page 17 Keith Hunter; page 18 Shannon Tofts; page 19 Keith Hunter; page 20 Keith Hunter; page 22 Keith Hunter; page 23 Nigel Young; page 24 Keith Hunter; page 25 Nigel Young; page 26 Keith Hunter; page 27 left Nigel Young; page 27 right Chris Hall; page 28 Richard Bryant / Arcaid; page 30 John Hewitt; page 31 bottom John Hewitt; page 32 top left John Hewitt; page 33 David Churchill; page 34 top Richard Bryant; page 34 bottom David Churchill; page 35 David Churchill; page 36 Innes Photographers; page 37 David Churchill; page 38 David Churchill; page 40 Peter Iain Campbell; page 41 top right Graeme Duncan; page 43 left David Churchill; page 43 Nigel Young; page 44 bottom Dennis Dornan; page 45 top Peter Iain Campbell; page 45 bottom Dennis Dornan; page 46 top Richard Bryant / Arcaid; page 46 bottom Peter Iain Campbell; page 47 Peter Iain Campbell; page 48 Tim Soar; page 49 bottom right Tim Soar; page 50 Tim Soar; page 51 Tim Soar; page 52 Tim Soar; page 53 Tim Soar; page 54 David Churchill; page 57 Nigel Young; page 60 Andrew Putler; page 61 Andrew Putler; page 62 Andrew Putler; page 64 Pixel Images; page 66 Pixel Images; page 78 Nigel Young; page 79 left Nigel Young; page 80 bottom Nigel Young; page 83 bottom Nigel Young; page 86 bottom Nigel Young; page 87 Nigel Young; page 88 Nigel Young; page 90 top centre The Peak Tower; page 90 bottom centre AMEC Developments; page 90 top right Andrew Putler; page 90 bottom right Peter Cook; page 91 top centre Colin Wade; page 91 centre Nigel Young; page 91 bottom centre Nigel Young; page 91 right Nigel Young; page 92 top left Nigel Young; page 92 top centre Andrew Putler / 3DD; page 92 centre Tim Soar; page 92 centre right Sean Gallagher; page 92 bottom right Andrew Putler; page 93 top left Virtual Artworks; page 93 centre left Andrew Putler; page 93 bottom left Andrew Putler; page 93 centre GMJ; page 93 top right Richard Bryant / Arcaid; page 93 bottom right Tom Kimbell; page 94 top left Andrew Putler; page 94 centre Andrew Putler; page 94 bottom centre Stuart Woods; page 94 centre right Anddrew Putler; page 94 bottom right Andrew Putler; page 95 top David Cruickshanks; page 95 main picture Shannon Tofts.